REA

Your Healing Journey Through Grief

A Practical Guide to Grief Management

by
Stanley Cornils

Robert D. Reed Publishers • San Francisco, CA

Robert D. Reed Publishers
750 La Playa, Suite 647
San Francisco, CA 94121
Phone: 650-994-6570 • Fax: -6579
E-mail: 4bobreed@msn.com
web site: www.rdrpublishers.com

Typesetter: **Barbara Kruger**
Cover Designer: **Julia Gaskill**

ISBN 1-931741-17-4

Library of Congress Catalog Control Number 2002102469

Manufactured, typeset and printed in the United States of America

Acknowledgements

The author is grateful for permission to reprint from the following books: *Mending,* Dorothy Hsu, ©1979, David C. Cook Publishing Co., used by permission of the author; *Beginnings,* Betty Jane Wylie, ©1982, 25 items on dealing with loneliness in Chapter 9, used by permission of Random House, Inc.; *Lonely, But Not Alone,* by Nicki Cruz, ©1981, "Mamie's Misery," used by permission of Zondervan Publishing Co.

Contents

Foreword

This is a very timely book. It deals with the subject of how grief can be managed, and it does so with many effective illustrations. It is the work of a well-trained and experienced pastor who has been a great help to a countless number of people.

At no point does it suggest that it is easy to deal with grief, but it does indicate that grief can be managed provided it is accepted wisely.

The heading of chapter one demonstrates how there is help for your grief, and the rest of the book gives hints on how grief must be faced and thus handled. The key is on page 16: "You cannot control what comes to you, but you can decide what you will do about it."

I recommend the book with enthusiasm!

Robert C. Leslie, Ph.D.
Emeritus Professor of Pastoral
 Psychology and Counseling
Pacific School of Religion
Berkeley, California

Introduction

If you are currently struggling with the trauma of losing a loved one by death or divorce, I know something about the sadness and hopelessness you are feeling, and I can say, "I know just how you feel because I have walked this path."

My wife and I weathered the sadness and disappointment of having our second child, Connie Jean, stillborn in 1946. That was a shaking experience, but God blessed us with another child, a son, three years later. My father died at the age of 64 during World War II. Travel was so restricted that I could not even purchase a bus ticket for the 1,000 mile trip to attend his funeral. That too, was a real loss and I missed the experience of being able to grieve with my mother, brothers and sisters. My mother passed away in her 86th year, and since then I have lost both a brother and two sisters. My wife and I have been happily married for more than half a century, and we have two grown sons and five wonderful grandchildren.

A long time ago, I learned in my experience as a Christian that God may not have planned that these losses should overtake me, but He has certainly permitted them. Long ago, I placed my life in His hands as well as the lives of my family, and whatever has happened, has the Lord's permission and, therefore, all is well. He will make it all "work together with all life's experiences for good," and He has (Romans 8:28).

One day as I was inviting a newly widowed lady to attend our Grief Recovery Seminar, she asked me if I were widowed. When I responded in the negative, she remarked, "Having never lost your mate, how can you help me work my way through my loss?" I answered, "The medical doctor who ministers to you in your illness does not have to have had the same disease you have in order to help you get well. What he needs to know is what to do to help you recover."

I do not claim to know all of the answers, but I do know some of the things that help grieving people get through the experience of losing a precious loved one.

Over more than fifty years of pastoral ministry, when someone became widowed or had lost a precious loved one or got divorced, I have always felt unqualified to minister to this kind of need. Ministering to grieving people was not adequately taught in most of the seminaries of my earlier days. How I wished that I might provide some kind of program for the grieving! But somehow I was always too busy with so many other things to do anything about this void in my ministry.

In the early 1960s, I began a diligent and serious study of the dynamics of the grief experience as a graduate student at Pacific School of Religion in Berkeley, California. At that time, the books on this subject written for the ordinary reader were very scarce. Why this was true is hard to understand in view of the fact that 5,480 people die in the course of a single day in our country—that's more than two million in the course of a year, yet so little had been written to help people recover from their grief. Death has been one of the matters most badly handled by most people.

During his lifetime, Sigmund Freud (1856-1939), the father of modern psychiatry, had written a great deal on this subject, but most of it was too technical for the average reader to understand.

Times have changed. In the 1940s, Eric Lindeman wrote *The Symptomatology and Management of Acute Grief* which was the outgrowth of the studies made following the Coconut Grove fire in Boston on November 28, 1942, in which almost 500 people lost their lives. This psychological data was the result of counseling sessions held by psychiatrists, psychologists, and other counselors with the survivors of that tragedy, their families and friends over a period of many months. This study has greatly influenced much of what has been written in this field since then.

During the past 25 years, there has been an abundance of books written for the widowed, the divorced, parents who have lost children, either before or after they were born, the survivors of suicide and murder, etc. Hardly a reputable publisher of general books exists in our country which does not have several titles in this field. This kind of interest in a very human problem is encouraging and long overdue since human beings have experienced grief since the day Cain slew his brother Abel.

As a result of my studies at PSR, I wrote *Managing Grief Wisely* in 1967. A gracious readership resulted in six printings. In 1990 I revised and expanded the text to produce *The Mourning After—How To Manage Grief Wisely.* For more than 20 years I have been conducting Grief Recovery Seminars in our area, where we talk about what grief does to people and some ways we can deal with these problems.

In the course of my studies, I discovered that with grieving people certain problems appeared to be common to most of them: The shock and numbness which stunned you when you learned your loved one had passed away; the denial of the fact; the dreadful and horrendous suffering during the first few months; the inability to accept the loss; the loneliness of having to adjust to a world from which your loved one was now missing; having to deal with anger and guilt; the dread that comes with the approach of a holiday season, a birthday or anniversary; money matters; and whatever else you are going to have to do in trying to get your life back on some normal track again.

Some years ago, Edi Munneke of Widowed Persons Service of American Association of Retired Persons wrote, "How I wish for a pattern or a recipe that I could hand to each newly widowed person and say, 'Follow this and your hurt will go away.'" Of course, I know that the hurt never really goes away, but I also know that **grief is not a disease which needs to be cured, but an experience which needs to be worked through by following a normal, natural mourning process which, if properly dealt with and completed, can result in a resourceful and constructive outcome so your life can go on and you won't hurt so much any more.** This is the thesis of my book. It is my aim to help you work it out in your own life. In outlining my Grief Recovery Seminars, I decided to deal principally with those problems which seem to be a part of most grieving people's experiences. This book is the text of the things we talk about together.

I am glad for the motivation which prompted you to begin reading this book. Stay with it to the end and put into practice some of the things we talk about, and you will be farther along toward recovering from your grief than if you had tried to do it on your own. You can learn to manage your grief rather than having it manage you. You can do more than survive.

A recipe card never cooked or baked anything by itself. You have to study it, decide what ingredients to get together, and then do it. In the same way, no road map ever took anyone on a trip. You decide where you want to go and then you consult the map to find out how to get there. I can assure you that two years down the road life will be different for you; you will be better, not bitter. The secret is to translate your knowledge into action. Work at it. It's a long and hard road but perseverance will pay off.

Some time ago, a young lady called and told me how she was suffering from the loss of a loved one. When I responded to her question about what went on in my seminars, she asked if I could take her grief away. I replied, "Neither I nor any group of persons can take your grief away. But we can share some things that will help you work your way through it and show you how you can go from a grief which you cannot handle to a grief which you can handle so you will be able to get on with your life."

You have to get yourself through your grief. There is no magic pill, there is no quick fix; no support group, no amount of information, no book, no counselor, no medication can get you through your grief. You have to get yourself through it. Others can point you in the right direction and share their experiences with you, but only you can take yourself in hand and move in the right direction. There is no substitute for action. People do not drown because they fall into the water; they drown because they do not fight back in an effort to save themselves.

I know that sounds arbitrary and like an open and shut case and you might want to argue the point, but the same principle is true in so many areas: Who is going to solve the alcoholic's problem? No alcoholic ever recovered from this addiction until he/she decided to do something about it. Who is going to lose weight? No overweight person ever lost weight and kept it off without the self-discipline of counting calories and practicing the most effective weight-loss exercises, like pushing one's self away from the table before eating more than one needs. Who is going to stop smoking? You have to stop smoking yourself. Others may help by giving support and encouragement, but you are the one who has to do the stopping: "What's going to be is up to me."

The same principle applies to grieving. You are the one who has to do something about it. And this, despite the fact that most people in the acute (suffering) stage of grief are not highly motivated to do anything. C.S. Lewis in his *A Grief Observed* referred to it as the "laziness of grief." Everything from the time you get up in the morning until you go back to bed at night is an effort and a drag, and it feels like your legs and feet are made of lead. Everything is just HARD to do and you could care less. Your friends keep telling you that "life must go on," but most of the time you wonder why.

When you lose a spouse or another special loved one, you crash land into a whole new world. This is the most difficult and challenging experience of your life. You may feel that your whole life has been ruined, you will never laugh again, and the rest of your days will be spent staggering along a pathway of sorrow. Others try to encourage us with words like "time heals all wounds." This is only partly true. The passing of time may lessen the impact of the loss and how it might affect our daily lives and thought, but grief does not automatically dissolve with the passage of time. It does no good to say, "I am just going to try to forget the whole thing ever happened." Judy Tatelbaum is the author of the statement: "Grieving is inevitable; recovering is not." There is something you have to do to resolve it to the point where you are recovering and life can continue to go on. Unresolved grief can last a lifetime, and it usually does.

A broken bone in the arm may heal without benefit of medical attention, but the arm may remain crooked because the bone had not been set and then immobilized until it healed, or the usefulness of some parts, like the fingers, might be impaired. If you have not faced up to and worked through the problems brought on by your loss, such as denial, anger, guilt, bitterness, hopelessness, fear of the future, loneliness, bewilderment, etc., the basic problems will not have been solved.

Grief is not an illness that needs to be cured but an experience which needs to be worked through. You will probably never get over it, but you can get through it. You won't forget your loss, but you won't dwell on it. Life will never be the same again, but that doesn't mean that it won't be worth living. There are few experiences in life which we cannot work our way through if we but find out what it is we need to do and then set about doing it. These are things this book is about.

In the May, 1986, issue of *Guideposts,* Lee Webber shares this helpful insight:

> I came to the swift raging river and the roar held the echo of fear;
> "Oh, Lord, give me wings to fly over,
> If you are as you promised quite near,"
> But He said, "Trust the grace I am giving,
> Far reaching (all pervasive), sufficient for you.
> Take my hand—we will face this together,
> But my plan is not over, but THROUGH."

The experiences of life never leave you where they found you. You will be different and some things will never be the same again, but life can still be good and beautiful.

The main purpose of this book is to share with grieving people the better ways of dealing with grief and to try to help them understand that what they are experiencing is normal and that it's okay to cry and be angry, even with God, and feel bewildered.

I am no Julia Child handing you a step-by-step recipe of suggested procedure, suggesting that you put all these things together in the right way and everything will come out beautifully. We must remember that each person's grief is unique. What helps one person might not be equally helpful to you. Along the way we will be faced with options and alternatives. Each one must choose what seems to be the most appropriate course of action or response.

As we proceed, I want to introduce you to some excellent books on the subject. In the bibliography at the end of my book, you will find more than 250 volumes listed in more than a dozen categories. In a sense, my approach is a cognitive one, based on knowledge of what professionals and non-professionals have found that really works. But knowledge alone is not enough; it must be translated into action. Believe me, there is a wealth of precious materials and ideas out there and they are yours for the taking and doing. How will you know whether or not they will work for you until you try them?

Understandably, because of your grief, your ability to concentrate on what you read is limited. This, too, is normal. Continue working on it and your capability to concentrate will improve.

After you have found some helpful things in my book, you might want to begin your own grief recovery group using it as a leader's guide as you study and heal together.

Finally, I want to introduce you to some wonderful people whom I have met over more than a decade of leading Grief Recovery Seminars. The accounts of their experiences are true—they really happened; only the names I have given them are fictitious. They are real and wonderful people, they have taught me so much, and I am so much richer for having known them.

THE MOURNER'S
(Applies especially to the

A. SHOCK

Numbness; disorder; panic; denial; like being in a trance; crying. (This is temporary– may last for hours, days, weeks.)

B. ACUTE STAGE – The suffering of grieving – These occur in no specific order – some not at all.

Anxiety episodes; mental pain; "I'm losing my mind"; frustration; sadness; fear; bitterness; insecurity; anger; irritability; crying; depression; helplessness; yearning and searching for the lost person; emptiness; "If only"; feeling isolated from others; difficulty in concentrating; guilt; hostility; self-pity; resentment toward others; inability to think clearly; confusion; L O N E L I N E S S; lack of awareness and judgment; blaming God; "Why me?"; loss of patterns of conduct; inability to accept reality; fatigue; hopelessness; heartache; visual and auditory proof that the loved one still lives and will return; withdrawal from others; fear of the future; inability to return to normal activities; bewilderment and much more!

LOWEST or TURNING POINT (not everyone's experience)

The choice we make: UP or DOWN

Resigning yourself to "poor me";
Chronic depression;
Anger towards self and others;
Physical, mental and emotional illness;
Low life satisfaction;
Unhappiness;
NO REAL RECOVERY!

PATH TO HEALING
Widowed and/or Divorced)

C. READJUSTMENT – recovery, resolution, acceptance – (one to two years or more from time of loss is normal.)

Getting on with living;
Reorganizing your life;
Renewed sense of well being;
Completing the grief work;
Discovering your independence;
Following up on dormant interests;
Building self-esteem: the cycle-self examination produces self-knowledge, which can beget self-esteem, which is necessary for self-confidence;
Setting and attaining new goals;
Trying new life patterns;
Forming new friendships and associations;
Joining support group;
Establishing new identity – self-worth;
Reassessing how things are now;
Accepting your new role as a "single";
"I will work my way through this!";
Accepting responsibility for yourself.

****

The circles in the path represent relapses into acute grieving brought on by an occurrence related to the memory of the loved one. They are periods when we regress and make no progress. They decrease in frequency and intensity as the grief work continues.

This chart is adapted and modified from another source (authorship unknown) by the author.

THE PATHWAY

1

The Healing Journey Through Grief

When death or divorce took your loved one away, you may have felt that your life had been sliced down the middle and you were left with the smaller half. The horror and hopelessness of the whole experience tempts you to run away, which sometimes is a good idea. But we cannot run forever. If you are a widow, you can appreciate the feelings of the East Indian widow who throws herself onto her husband's funeral pyre. The practice is called suttee. In years past, many widows actually did this, but it is now forbidden by law. There are better ways of facing widowhood. We do not honor the dead by dying with them.

Following the moment when someone told you that your loved one had passed away, a host of undesirable, repugnant and unsavory guests forced their way into your consciousness. They are the negative and difficult emotions listed under B on the chart—the suffering stage, and they have come to live with you unbidden. Not a single one is easy to live with. Some will stay for a short while; others will be your uninvited guests for a long time, and some will never leave you. What an invasion!

The Path

Now look at the diagram on the preceding pages. Study it awhile. It is not a timetable for getting through one's grief, but a listing of experiences and emotions which may come to a person in grief. All of them are normal when they occur within reasonable limits. It's a dark and dismal picture, to be sure. The mourner's path is a long and mapless road which you did not choose. It is a dark, dismal, and confusing picture indeed!

Paths are not for looking at or sitting down on, but for walking on. They are made to help us go from one place to another. In studying this path, you are looking not for ways to circumvent your grief but for ways of getting from a grief which you cannot handle to a way of grieving which you can handle and then going on with your life.

Certainly you did not choose this path, except that the seeds of this experience were sown on your wedding day when you said "I do" to the promise that you would love, honor, and cherish your loved one "until death do us part." Charles Allen in *God's Psychiatry* states: "Grief is the price tag we find on the package of love." The possibility of your walking this path has been there since your wedding day. You just did not know when.

There are some problems in life that are impossible to solve, but they can be made manageable. Just because you have the problem does not mean that nothing in your life is ever going to be right again. The loss of a mate is one of the most stressful events in life, but even a problem as big as this can be made manageable.

What to Do

What do you do when you have arthritis? You suffer with it! You can do some things to reduce the pain, but basically you suffer with it. Similarly, if a problem cannot be eliminated, it is hoped that you learn how to live with it. And so it is with grief. If you don't learn how to manage it, it will manage *you* and control your whole outlook on life. Sadness will rule.

That is not the best way to handle your grief. You can learn some kind of control, even though it may not be complete. You may never get over your grief, but you can learn how to handle it so your life can go on. Life will never be the same again. You will always have your memories. Right now the worst thing you can do is to do *nothing*. If you really try, you will discover you can do more than you thought you could.

Adapting

When you lose your mate, you have to take on some new responsibilities. If you are a widow, you have to assume some duties your husband performed—like getting the wheels rotated on the car, having it lubricated, getting the oil changed, having the radiator flushed out, etc. If you are a widower, the same things apply to household chores—cooking, washing, cleaning, etc. Even though the new tasks may seem formidable and disheartening, what are the alternatives? Let the car fall into disrepair, don't eat, wear dirty clothes and watch your home getting messier with each passing day?

For the widow who has second thoughts about "man chores," you really don't have to do it all yourself. You can take the car to the service station every month and tell the mechanic to give it the works, whatever it needs. Certain mechanics might also give your pocketbook the works, selling you things your car doesn't need. Learning to deal with mechanics can be an exciting experience. Read Mary Jackson's book *Greaseless Guide to Car Care*. She will tell you how to talk with mechanics.

The same thing is true of the widower who has to become familiar with household duties, such as cooking, keeping the house clean, grocery shopping, etc. Learn everything you can about your new duties, and you will be able to deal more constructively with them.

A prominent doctor who treats cancer patients in one of our local hospitals recently made this statement in a newspaper interview: "People who are terminally ill or who have had radical surgery need to learn how to live with their illness, and I make it a point to apprise them of what they can expect down the road." That's telling it like it is, and in most cases, this might be the best approach. However, because we are all different and each one of us has his or her own way of handling the crises of life, it might not be the wisest approach for each patient. Some doctors even go so far as to tell a patient how long they might expect to live. In my opinion, no doctor should do this; it might become a self-fulfilling prophecy.

Some patients would be devastated by the doctor's prophecy. They wouldn't even try to cooperate with his treatment. They might just give up, lie down and await the sweet messenger of death. If the patient really wants to know how long he or she might live, the doctor might say as a challenge, "That pretty much depends upon you. If you have the courage and strength to fight this disease, you might just win many more years for yourself."

There are countless instances on record of patients who made it their mission to beat the doctor's odds. They realize that his M.D. degree signifies that he is a doctor of medicine and not a minor deity. Thousands of people have lived many years beyond extreme and violent surgical procedures. An increasingly large number of cancer patients experience remission and live out their normal life spans; they simply refuse to die on a doctor's order.

The experience of losing a loved one by death or divorce is very much like that of a recovery from surgery or illness. It's a long, arduous task, filled with hard work and diligence. Most people eventually recover from bereavement. They never forget their loved one, but they do get through their grief, and so can you.

That's what this <u>Path Through Grief</u> is all about. It tries to show you what is down the road, so you won't complain, "Why didn't someone tell me it was going to be like this?" It does not guarantee that if you start from Point A and touch all the bases through C (readjustment on the top right of the chart), you will have won the battle and your grief will be healed. It doesn't happen that way, because the path through grief is not lineal, but zigzag. There is no steady progression from grief to non-grief. There are peaks and valleys. Grief is not an orderly process. Many of the negative emotions which we experience seem to be going on at the same time: anger, guilt, depression, remorse, hopelessness and loneliness. It's very much like trying to ride out a tornado. Each of us is different and has our own timetable in dealing with the experience.

I'm not very comfortable with suggesting that there are stages in the grieving process. I do believe we can be aware that there are at least three basic and noticeable points involved: (A) SHOCK; (B) SUFFERING— The Acute Stage; (C) READJUSTMENT—Acceptance or Recovery. Just as in a surgical procedure, there is the shock of the experience during which the patient may be little aware of what is going on. When consciousness returns, there is pain and suffering. And finally there is recovery. As we recuperate from accidents, surgery or illness, so we recover from the other traumas of life, including the worst of all, the loss of a loved one.

There is some comfort to be gained in knowing that there are stages. The term implies that eventually there will be a final stage beyond which you will be able to get on with your life, even though that may seem a long way from where you are right now.

A. Shock

When someone told you your loved one had died, you crash-landed into a whole new world which you never expected to see or experience. Everything seemed upside down, inside out, unreal, as though your whole world had come to an end. You were in a state of shock. There was a numbness, disorder, panic, inability to believe it had really happened. You told yourself, "I'm dreaming, and someday I will wake up and find this isn't real." It was like being in a trance. Tears came uncontrolled. You were in utter despair. Perhaps others had to do for you what you could not do for yourself: calling the funeral home, planning the service, purchasing a cemetery plot, etc. And all this occurring while you were almost totally unaware of what was going on, too stricken to function.

Too often tranquilizing drugs are administered to a person going through this experience in the belief that it will help him or her. Ironically, many people feel later on that they were cheated rather than spared. There is some truth to the saying, "You must feel if you are going to heal." The use of drugs can prevent the feelings necessary for grief work to begin. It is more therapeutic to be a participant rather than a desensitized spectator. Most of us profit more by being awake and conscious through it all. In some ways, this state of seeming unconsciousness is a mercy and a blessing. It's very much like the effect of a severe injury or disease which results in such excruciating pain—if it were not turned off into unconsciousness, it would be fatal.

The only mourners who might be spared the experience of shock are those whose loved one passed away following a lengthy illness. For weeks or months they may have been dealing with anticipatory grief and so have already traveled part of the pathway. However, very few people are really prepared for the death of a loved one no matter how long they may have anticipated it. When it finally does happen, they are almost as emotionally devastated as if they had no warning.

A state of shock may last only a few hours. For some it may be days before the real nature of things begins to appear. Unfortunately, there are others for whom this tragic condition may continue for several months. For many, it may recur in the months that follow.

Down the left side of the chart you will notice circles which are spaced intermittently along the way. These indicate relapses. I think most of us would agree that grief is cruel. Why doesn't it hit us just once and then go away and leave us alone to heal? Every novice in this fellowship of suffering knows that it doesn't work this way. It keeps coming back to hit us again and again.

You may be congratulating yourself on your recent progress; you haven't felt the need to go to the cemetery for the past week. In general, things seem to be on the upgrade and you're feeling good about your progress. Then something unexpected and dreadful happens: A personal letter addressed to your loved one is delivered, sent by someone who didn't know about the death; you accidentally come across some special memento charged with deep feelings for your loved one; someone makes a remark which opens the wound. Suddenly and without warning, you are back into the despair of acute grieving. All your progress seems to have vanished. Heartbreak and dismay take over. How disheartening and upsetting! You think to yourself, "I went forward three steps, then fell back two—I'll never get through this."

These relapses into painful grieving and going around in a circle of self-pity are normal to most people traveling this road, and you are not to blame yourself for regressing temporarily. You didn't cause it. What brought it on was a heavy blow striking you on a very sore spot which was trying to heal. These relapses may last a matter of minutes, hours, or may even spoil the bigger part of a week for you. Eventually, you will pick yourself up and get back on the road again. Remember, this is normal. When relapses occur we may have the tendency to believe that we are going nowhere but crazy. Remember—not many things in life proceed perfectly.

The best thing to do when a relapse occurs is to spend some effort by taking the offensive: Go to lunch with someone, go shopping, get out of the house for a while, leave town, have a good cry, make it a real pity party, or help someone who needs you. **You will find that when you help someone out of a hole (depression, problem, difficulty, etc.), you will, without even trying, bury some of your own problems in that hole. This is a miracle. But God does not perform it. He has reserved it for you.** Only you can do it. Dry your tears and count your blessings instead of your burdens.

There is good news. Notice that the circles (relapses) drawn into the pathway at the beginning are boldly outlined and occur more frequently in the early stages. As you move along, they become farther apart and less intense in their impact. Eventually they disappear. But don't be disheartened if you experience one or more of them in the second or third year of your loss.

B. The Acute Stage—Suffering

Just as in the experience following surgery, after unconsciousness and numbness wears off, pain and suffering set in. When you lost your loved one, the door of your consciousness automatically opened and a host of uninvited and unwelcomed visitors came in to live with you. Hopefully, some of them will be with you for only a short time; others will stay longer and some will be with you as long as you live. Notice the long list of negative emotional experiences listed in this section. As a grieving person, you are a candidate for any one or a combination of them. What a collection of impressive and frightening negatives! What an emotional mob scene—a real patch of weeds! The picture of grief is painted in many colors, most of them somber and dark. Many of these emotions you have already experienced. Hopefully, some of them will not be yours. They appear in no special order. All of them within reasonable limits are normal. You are not losing your mind. Notice that "loneliness" is emphasized. It is the most common experience for people who have lost a significant loved one.

Some problems we encounter in life seem to have no solutions, but they can be made manageable. That is where grief support groups come in, and that is how we can learn to cope. Falling into the water does not drown a person; staying there without fighting back results in drowning. When you choose to act, you become an agent of life rather than a victim.

Right now, the place of readjustment seems so far away. It's a vague dream, a figment of the imagination. But you can find it by doing your grief work and then realize that it was more than a dream away. There is help for your grief. Most of it is at the end of your arm, but you have to work it out yourself. John James in *The Grief Recovery Handbook* says, "No book or counselor, friend or support group can recover you from grief. Only you can recover yourself."

Whatever the variety of emotions we experience, if we try to understand them and realize that they are normal, we may learn how to cope with them.

Notice, about two-thirds of the way down the left side of the chart, the "Lowest" or "Turning Point." For some very fortunate people, this point is not on their itinerary. They never have to make the decision about whether they will go on and work their way through their grief, because they have always met the crises of life in positive and practical ways. They have learned how to accept the unacceptable and surmount the insurmountable. They are the well-adjusted ones and definitely a minority. They, and all who know them, realize that they will make it because they have developed a positive response to all of life's difficulties. No one worries about them. This does not mean that they do not grieve, because they do. But they have learned how to deal constructively with whatever life hands to them—a rare breed, to be sure.

In order for a turning point to occur, someone or something has to change. This happened to Mary Ellen as she shared the experiences of her widowhood with a group: "One day I just sat down and made up my mind. I decided he is not here, but I am. He is dead but I am alive, so I'm going to do whatever I can to get on with my life. That's why I joined this support group." And she did get on with her life.

C. Readjustment

What you do or don't do about your grief depends on you. It's not a "can" or "cannot" situation, but rather a "will" or "will not" proposition.

Making the decision to go on could be the most challenging and important undertaking of your life.

Up to this point, the grieving person has been in what a parachutist would call a "free fall": no control, and the only direction is down. Once the parachute has opened, there is an element of control. The experienced parachutist can, in large part, direct and guide the descent and land on the target, and so can you.

A person may be in a free fall for weeks or months without apparent direction or control and then one day make the decision, "I'm going to work my way through this." Now the parachute is open. This marks a turning point, a new direction, and a new experience.

Not every grieving person comes to this decision or turning point. They drift along like a tumbleweed in the desert being pushed around by every passing wind (the emotions of suffering). They have no motivating power within them to control their direction. They shut out the world, pull the covers over their heads, and dwell on yesterdays and what used to be. They never make the turn into the upward path toward recovery. They continue on a downward spiral. They will not learn how to fight back. For the rest of life, they continue in their grief with NO REAL RECOVERY. I'm sure you know someone who fits this picture.

Even though we don't normally think of mourning as a process of recovery, there can be no recovery without it. Every person who consciously or unconsciously decides, "I will work my way through this" moves on to the other side and begins the upward climb. Sadness begins to subside, memories are easier to live with, even pleasant. You can laugh again, and normal activities resume. It sounds easy, but it isn't. There just is no simple, easy way through grief. It's a long, hard, painful and repetitious climb. But the dividends are compounded daily. It's worth it! After all, what is the alternative? NO REAL RECOVERY.

I assure you that if I could tear off two years from the calendar and transplant you to that point of recovery, you would feel different and better, so many things will have changed. Accept your new role as a "single." Establish a new identity. Reach out by forming new friendships and interests, experiment with new life patterns. Set new goals. Do some things you've always wanted to do. Follow up some long-suppressed interests. Complete your grief work. Join a support group. Many studies indicate that if we have a focus outside ourselves, it will help us survive the crises of life.

Instead of allowing your thoughts to be directed inwardly in self-pity, volunteer your services to help others who are less fortunate than you are, or to the many causes which depend on volunteers to keep them going.

Build a new self-esteem and self-worth. The equation goes like this: Self-examination produces self-knowledge, which begets self-esteem, which is necessary for self-confidence. Readjustment will come. Grief work hurts, but it works. It's painful, but it pays.

While you may grieve because of a loss, you can keep yourself from losing the perspective and appreciation for the many good things that can still happen in your life. It was Helen Keller who said, "When one door closes, another opens, but often we look so long at the closed door that we do not see the one which has opened for us."

You can do more than survive. You can emerge as a better person if you will really work at it. The worst thing you can do is nothing.

Comparatively speaking, there are not many things in this world which are impossible. According to the older laws of aerodynamics, the bumblebee cannot fly because its fuselage is too big for its wing area. Fortunately, the bumblebee doesn't know this—he just flies.

I have the confidence that you will never meet anything you can't handle. You may not believe this now, but if you will apply all the resources at your disposal, including those within yourself, you will discover it. Courage isn't so much having the strength to go on—it's going on when you don't have the strength.

How long does all this take? It depends on how well and completely you work on it. The route one takes on the pathway does not depend on "can" or "cannot," but on "will" or "will not."

You are now faced with the most demanding undertaking of your life. Any good that may come to you in the future will depend more on you than on anyone else. If you are willing to work your way, there can be an end to sorrow, and your life can go on and be meaningful again. It is not what happens to you, but what you do about it that determines the outcome. Happiness depends more on ourselves than on the circumstances of our lives. You cannot control what comes to you, but you can decide what you will do about it. You will never get over it, but you CAN get *through* it. Commit yourself to life.

THIS TOO SHALL

There is a legend about David, the king of Israel, regarding the fact that he was a man of many moods. The Bible notes that during periods of great depression he would call musicians in to play for him until the mood passed.

One day he summoned the palace jeweler and gave him the following order: "Fashion for me a ring and on it inscribe words that will lift me up when I am depressed and when I am exalted and joyous it will bring me down to basic realities. There must be but one inscription for both joy and sorrow."

The Jeweler pondered the order for months, but no inspiration came. One day he met Solomon, the king's son, in the palace garden and shared his father's order with him. Almost immediately Solomon replied: "Inscribe these words on the ring: Gem Zu Ya-avor **(this too shall pass)**. Both sorrow and joy are not forever."

2

The Key to Recovery
The Four Tasks of Mourning

Ballpark Rules

It is the last half of the ninth inning of the baseball game at the park. Two batters have struck out. The score is 5 to 5, with no one on base. The atmosphere is charged. The third batter steps to the plate and hits a home run. The fans stand and cheer as he saunters around the diamond, but after he touches home plate, the numbers on the scoreboard still indicate that the score is 5 to 5. The fans are perplexed and begin to murmur and boo. The umpire steps out and announces to the crowd, "The runner failed to touch second base; the score is disallowed."

In most instances of delayed grief or symptoms, or incomplete grieving (being stuck in grief), the counselor could almost be certain that one or more of the four basic tasks of grieving had not been properly dealt with.

Big Order

When you are faced with a new job that you've never done before, or have to move to another city because of your work, or face a surgical procedure, it's normal to have misgivings and even to be afraid. And what makes matters worse is that it's all cut and dried—you have to go along with it! One of your first temptations might be to run away, but here it is in front of you and you must deal with it.

Your employer offers you a more responsible position but your lack of self-esteem makes you question your ability. The company is moving to another state. The doctor decides that surgery is the only remedy. These are some instances in which fear is warranted.

The same sort of situation faces you when you have lost a loved one by death or divorce. You cannot change the fact. You have to deal with the loss. It may be a new experience for you.

There are few things as frightening as the unknown. Ignorance breeds fear, but knowledge leads to understanding. The more we can read about and study what we are facing and talk with others who have had similar experiences, the more we will be able to understand and deal constructively with it.

In the San Francisco Bay Area, Dr. Dean Edell is featured on ABC radio and television giving medical advice. He is a very knowledgeable doctor. I once heard him say, "If you are ill and your doctor examines you and subjects you to certain tests, he will then give you his diagnosis. Let us say he informs you that you have diabetes and proceeds to share with you the type of treatment he will pursue. You should then go to the reference desk of your local library and check out a medical textbook which lists medical diseases and their treatment. Turn to the section on diabetes and read what it says. You will probably learn more about diabetes than you really wanted to know, but in gaining knowledge you will understand why your doctor is following a certain pattern of treatment. You will not only be helping yourself in understanding your ailment, but you will also be more cooperative and hopeful in going along with his treatment."

What If?

But what if you are told that there is no medical or surgical treatment for your ailment? You are advised that you are just going to have to learn to live with it, through diet, exercise, etc. In the same way, grief resulting from the loss of a loved one is something which must be worked through and which you can learn to live with. However, expecting total resolution of your grief is a false goal and very seldom occurs. Some aspects of your loss might never go away permanently. You can learn to live with them.

Things might be so bad with you right now that you cannot believe any kind of recovery is possible. You are certain that you will never laugh again or even tell a funny story. Yet look around you and note the many people who also have lost loved ones and who appear to have recovered. You want to be like them, but you might not have the foggiest idea on how to go about it.

People who are grieving the loss of a loved one by death or divorce do want to recover. But how? Judy Tatelbaum in *You Don't Have to Suffer* makes the statement: "Grieving is inevitable, but recovering is not." So here you are, standing before a gigantic door marked "To Recovery," but it's locked and you have no key. Take my word for it—recovery IS on the other side of that door, and you have the ability to get the key.

Good News—Bad News

There is a key to recovery, but you must make it yourself. It cannot be purchased from the hardware store. You will not need to attend a locksmith school, nor will you need any special tools. Good counsel and directions will provide the pattern you follow. Anyone can do it if they really want to. Others have and so can you.

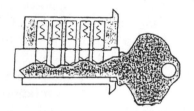

The cylinder lock contains a number of tumblers or pins, little rods of various lengths. Each is spring-loaded to keep the tumbler resting in the notch ground into the key. When the key is inserted into the lock, the bottoms of the tumblers rest in the valleys cut into the key and the tumblers will line up in a straight line. Then all you have to do is turn the knob of the door and it will open. There is no other proper way of opening it, and no other key will cause the tumblers to line up.

Here is the pattern for the key to the door which leads to recovery: FOUR BASIC TASKS MUST BE ACCOMPLISHED IN ORDER FOR SUCCESSFUL RECOVERY FROM GRIEF TO OCCUR. A delineation and amplification of this outline may be found in *Grief Counseling and Grief Therapy* by J. William Worden and also in Therese Rando's *Grieving: How to Go On Living When Someone You Love Dies*. The concept is as true to life and experience as if you had found it in the Holy Bible.

Task 1: You Need to Accept the Reality of the Loss

When a loved one has died and we are still in shock, it is normal to feel that the death really did not occur. We think to ourselves, "This is a mistake. It really did not happen. Sometime I will wake up and discover that it was all a nightmare." The benefits of funerary rites are more for the living than for the dead. The ultimate proof of death is a lifeless body. Maybe that is why we spend so much time, energy, and money to recover bodies after airplane crashes, accidents, drownings, and earthquakes. Our hearts need that ultimate proof before we can go on. When we see the body and talk to it, there is no answer. When we reach out and touch it, it is cold. We have come face to face with reality. This is the opposite of denial. We acknowledge the death. We accept the fact that the person has died. The physical fact is irreversible, and what we cannot change we might as well accept.

One of the meanings of the word "accept" is "to receive without protest." This might not occur during the early stages of your grief, and for some it might never occur. Probably it would be more correct to say that in the early phases we "acknowledge" that death has occurred. You will discover in the chapter on acceptance that death has occurred. You will also discover that acceptance might not occur until after you have made a decision to go on with your life and have crossed over to the creative side of the Healing Journey chart and begun to do the things which will lead toward readjustment, recovery, and resolution.

This kind of verification is denied the loved ones of those who are Missing in Action (MIA). In many instances we might need clarification on how the death occurred. If the loved one was killed in an accident, we will not be satisfied until we have gone to see the place where the accident occurred. The father of a young man who gave his life in the war could not rest until he had gone to the military cemetery in a foreign country and read his son's name on a headstone. Our national memorial, known as the Vietnam Wall, serves much the same purpose for grieving relatives. Parents who lose a baby to Sudden Infant Death Syndrome (SIDS) never have the satisfaction of knowing why their child died, because medical science has not yet been able to identify the physiological components of this silent baby killer.

So the first notch we need to cut in our key to recovery is to do whatever we can to acknowledge the death and accept the fact that the loved one is gone and will not return.

Non-Acceptance

Historians tell us that when Queen Victoria's husband, Prince Albert, died, she refused to accept the fact. She gave orders to his valet to put out the clothing he would wear each morning, draw his bath and arrange his shaving equipment, and there was always a place setting for him at the table as if he were still alive.

Any parent who has lost a child might want to leave the child's room "just as he left it." This may be acceptable to fill a need for the short term, but if continued indefinitely, it is a form of denial.

Many a widower has made the decision to leave everything in the home just as it was on the day his wife died. That's a beautiful sentiment and a tribute to the lost loved one, and no one would deny you the right to have things "as they were" for a few months, but it's also a sure way to get stuck in one's grief, and when you're stuck, you're not making progress. Putting a period at the end of our loved one's life will enable us to go on with our own.

Task 2: You Need to Experience the Pain of Grief

In simplest terms, this means that when you need to cry, just cry. To many people, giving way to grief is stigmatized as morbid, unhealthy, and demoralizing. Actually, the opposite is true. Take a lesson from your body. When you cut yourself, you bleed. This is the body's way of cleaning the wound so it can heal. Sometimes, in an effort to avoid the pain, we run away and take flight. We take trip after trip, always seeing new things and meeting new people. We shun people and places that would remind us of our loss. But you can't run forever. You will always have to come back. There is no way to avoid working our way through this painful experience if we are ever going to get beyond it. You cannot run away from the problems any more than you can outrun your shadow.

Elizabeth Harper Neeld in *Seven Choices* reminds us that we need to choose to give ourselves permission to experience and express our grief. We decide whether we will experience and express our grief or stifle and suppress our responses to it.

She cites seven reasons why we might choose not to express our grief:

1. The pain might seem unbearable.
2. It may seem more reasonable, since nothing can be done about the loss, to try to forget it—to put it behind us as quickly as possible.
3. People around us may encourage us to "be brave, be strong, pull ourselves together."
4. Or we may feel that if we don't rise above the loss, we are denying tenets of faith or a philosophy we have affirmed and lived by.
5. Perhaps people around us may indicate, and we ourselves may believe, that sufficient time has passed for us to be finished with our grieving.
6. We might be embarrassed to express our grief in front of others.
7. We might fear we are going crazy because we curtail the expression of our grief because it is interfering with our daily activities.

She goes on, "We don't want to be overcome by rushes of sorrow and lose control. We don't want to stare into the emptiness of the black abyss. We don't want to open ourselves to hurt. <u>And until we know that</u> <u>there is a natural, normal mourning process that can culminate in a</u> <u>constructive outcome, this intense grieving is necessary for the</u> <u>beginning of that process, we have little incentive to choose to</u> <u>experience the pain.</u>

Drugs

Not infrequently, doctors and well-meaning friends will prescribe drugs to help us through our grief. Drugs do not cure this problem or make it go away; they only deaden our sensitivity to the loss. One widow who was "really out of it" on the day of her husband's funeral said, "As I looked down on my husband in the casket, I was so fogged up with medication that inside I was as dead as he was." Some kind of help in getting to sleep at night might be in order for many people, for unless you get a good night's sleep you're just not ready to meet the demands of a new day. But don't become dependent on sleeping aids.

Task 3: You Need to Adjust to Living in the World from Which Your Loved One Is Now Absent

This takes patience and practice. It is achieved painfully, step by step, as you gradually come to grips with the fact that your loved one is no longer in your life as he or she was before.

Mazie achieved this very early in her widowhood. Three months before her husband passed away, they had purchased tickets for an extended trip. After he died, she had to make a decision about the trip. Happily, she decided to take it and invited her 18-year-old granddaughter to accompany her.

On their first night out, as they walked into their hotel room, she put her suitcase on the floor and tossed her handbag on the bed. Then the thought struck her, "What am I doing here?" Almost as quickly the answer came, "That's the way it's going to be from here on out." She shared with our group that that was the biggest turning point in her widowhood.

Death brings many changes. It is very difficult to realize how important a person is to us until that person is taken from us, then one discovers the many roles he or she played. For the first time in many years you now have to take care of yourself and many other things. Your mate is no longer there to support and advise you. Who will take care of the car and the repairs around the house? You cook meals which you now have to eat alone. You make the bed every day, knowing that you will be sleeping in it alone. Each time something goes wrong or breaks, you are reminded that he is not there to fix it.

The death of Gloria's husband opened her eyes very quickly to this fact. Before he died, she had never written a check. One of her friends showed her how to do it, but she always did the book work and check-writing in the solitude and quietness of her own home, as she was dreadfully afraid of making a mistake. Then one day she had to pick up a prescription at the pharmacy. When she stepped up to the cash register, she realized she had only a small amount of cash with her, not nearly enough to pay the bill. But she had her checkbook. Consternation! For the first time in the presence of a lot of witnesses, she pulled herself together and wrote the check. She said she walked out of the store strutting like she had just won the gold at the Olympics. Lucky for her that she was forced into that turning point. The check cleared the bank and was returned to her. She even had thoughts of framing it and hanging it on the wall. After that, writing a check was not a big deal. We are going to have to work hard at getting accustomed to the world without our loved one. No one promises us that we will like it, but we don't have a choice or maybe we do. J. William Worden in *Grief Counseling and Grief Therapy* says this: "The aborting of Task 3 is not adapting to the loss. People work against themselves by promoting their own helplessness, by not developing the skills they need to cope, or by withdrawing from the world and not facing up to environmental requirements. However, most people do not take this negative course. They usually decide that they must fill the roles to which they are unaccustomed and develop skills they never had." This is not easy, but it is not impossible. You can do it!

Task 4: You Must Withdraw the Emotional Energy Which You Expended on the Person You Lost and Re-invest It in Another Relationship: a Person, a Cause, New Activities, New Roles in Your Life, New Hopes and Beliefs, an Object, Becoming a Volunteer, Etc.

This task is fundamental to recovery and will probably be the most difficult to perform. It might take the longest time to complete, because it involves changes you will be making in your relationship with the person who died. At first glance this sounds almost callous and brutal. It does not mean that we heartlessly turn our back to all the beautiful memories and experiences we had with our loved one. It does mean that we begin to gently close the door to the past just a little bit as we set ourselves to forming new and creative relationships. If you do not complete this assignment, you might later see that your life actually stopped when your loved one died. Some grievers say that it takes four full seasons of a year before grief begins to abate.

At first glance, it would appear to many survivors that fulfilling this requirement would be dishonoring the memory of the deceased and would amount to betrayal. But wouldn't your loved one want you to move on rather than walk the hallways of grief for the rest of your life?

Many survivors are frightened about making another investment in anything new or anyone else for fear that they will suffer loss again, so they vow that they will never fall in love again. No one is ever too old to fall in love. Still others feel that they were married for time and eternity and therefore they could not wholeheartedly love another. It seems to me that when death occurs the marriage contract is fulfilled or completed.

If you are having a problem with Task 4, you have a great deal of company. To help you along, I would like to suggest that you think about and contemplate what William James, a renowned American psychologist (1842-1910), said: "The greatest discovery of my generation is that people can alter the circumstances of their lives if they will but alter their attitudes." Only you can alter your attitudes. Fulfilling this task does not mean that you are trying to forget the loved one or that you will no longer love him or her.

Worden recounts the story of a teenage girl whose father had died. Adjusting to this loss was very difficult. "As she began to move through to the other side of Task 4 (recovering by forming new relationships), she wrote a note to her mother from college in which she articulated what many people come to realize when they are grappling with emotional withdrawal and re-investment. "There are other people to be loved, and it doesn't mean that I love my dad any less."

Therese Rando, in speaking to a widow, offers this good counsel: "You must let go of being connected to him as if he were still alive. The emotional energy that went into your relationship with him gradually must be detached from him, since he can no longer return it. In time, it must be channeled elsewhere where it can be returned for your emotional satisfaction."

Difficult as it is to perform, Task 4 can be accomplished. It may take six months or as long as several years, and a lot of real work, to move through this task and come out a whole person ready to take up life again. Don't isolate or insulate yourself from the rest of the world. Become interested in other people and things. Each day that you survive you will be one step nearer recovery and readjustment. You will never see and experience the beauty of the distant shore unless you are willing to pull away from the shore you are on now. However long it takes, when you are sure the processes of grief have been addressed and completed as much as possible as you understand them, you will be better and will feel better about yourself.

Example

The following story out of my own pastoral experience relates how one couple completed their Task 4: Clinton was the only child of his parents. In the spring of 1940, he graduated with honors from the UCLA Medical School and was awaiting the start of his internship in the fall. In June he was on a mountain-hiking trip with his Boy Scout troop. Somehow, somewhere up the mountainside, a large stone became dislodged and almost noiselessly started down the steep grade. None of the Scouts saw it coming, but when it sailed across the trail it struck Clinton in the head and killed him instantly.

Can you imagine the grief of his parents? How many hopes and dreams evaporated for them that day! For many parents it might have been the end of any reason for living. But not for this good Christian couple. Somewhere in their experience they had learned that life in this world is not always fair and does not give us any guarantees, only options, alternatives, and choices. We cannot control what life brings us, but we can and do determine what we will do with what comes.

Before the beginning of the fall semester at UCLA Medical School that year, these parents presented themselves at the admissions office of the school where most people had known their son. They offered to pay all the expenses for a student who was qualified to pursue a career in medicine but lacked the funds to make it possible. Of course, they asked to meet that person before they gave their approval for the arrangement. What an example of Task 4!

This couple did not just write a check twice a year to pay a bill; they had this student in their home throughout the course of each year. They shared holidays and mid-term breaks together. They entertained the student in their home. That student became like an adopted child. I don't know how many deserving young people they helped in this way through the years, but I do know that before they were finished with life, instead of having just one son, they had a whole family of medical students and doctors around their family table when they sat down for a holiday dinner.

I am aware that certainly there are many other things which help people recover from their grief. Whenever you find them, use them. I know that these four tasks are fundamental, the foundation upon which you will be able to function and speed your own recovery.

In every way possible, try to understand the processes of grief, address them, and complete them as far as you can. Life will be better, rather than bitter, for you.

3

Acceptance

Death—A Fact of Life

Death is a very common occurrence in our world. In the United States more than 5,000 people die in the course of a day—that's more than two million a year. Sometimes we need to remind ourselves that in our world all living things are dying things. **Everything that is alive today will someday be dead, and that includes you and me.** Nothing on this planet will live forever. I don't like it, but I cannot change it. As obvious and universal as death is, the number of people who have difficulty accepting it is truly impressive; if you are having difficulty with this, you are not abnormal. You have a great deal of company.

The First Step

For emphasis I repeat the words of William James, the eminent American psychologist of the 19th century: **"The acceptance of what has happened is the first step to overcoming the consequences of any misfortune."** Acceptance seems so simple and obvious that we might assume that it would not take any great effort. But that's not the way it really is. Not infrequently, when news comes to us that a loved one has died, we might attempt to deny the fact: "Someone made a mistake; it really didn't happen; they sent the wrong message; sometime I'll wake up and discover that it was only a horrible dream." Yes, acceptance is difficult for many who are bereaved.

Burial rites can be helpful in this respect. The body has been removed to a funeral home; it has been embalmed and placed in a casket; there may be a visitation or a wake with friends and family; you look and you touch—the lifeless body is the ultimate reality at this point. Then there is a funeral or memorial service, followed by a trip to the cemetery where the body is buried or entombed, or cremains are interred or scattered.

All these elements help us acknowledge the death, at least intellectually. A more complete emotional acceptance may come later, or at the point where we decide that life must and will go on without the loved one and we move in that direction.

Caroline McKendricks spoke for many of us when she said, following the death of her mother: "My mind says I must accept the fact of the loss, and I do, but my heart can't go along with it—it keeps saying 'NO.'"

There is a distinction between intellectual acknowledgment and emotional acceptance. After we have gone through all the leave-taking and rites of passage for our loved one, our mind should be convinced that he or she has died. We intellectually acknowledge it. This does not mean total acceptance, because in our heart we might still be crying "NO."

Remember?

If you have been widowed, it might sound cruel for me to say that the seeds of your widowhood were sown by you on your wedding day. Do you remember the words "until death do us part" or "so long as we both shall live"? Of course, you were not thinking of the full meaning of those words at the time, but deep inside you knew that marriage was to last a lifetime and then one day either you or your spouse would lay the other into the arms of God. The marriage contract will then have been completed. That is just a fact of life. Someone who decides never to marry will never be widowed.

There are some people who make the considered decision never to fall in love because they feel they could not live through the experience of having to say goodbye. Grief is a part of the price we pay for love. It was J. Bratner who said, "Only people who avoid love can avoid grief." Even making the decision never to fall in love has its price. If you live to a ripe old age, you will have no grandchildren and might have nothing more than a pussycat on your lap.

No Guarantees

Life does not come with guarantees—only options and alternatives, choices we make. No one who marries knows whether or not that marriage will last a lifetime, or whether they will have children who will live long enough to make them a grandparent. Rabbi Harold Kushner, who wrote *When Bad Things Happen to Good People,* is a leading scholar in the field of grief management. He was told when his firstborn, Aaron, was three that the boy had a rare disease which produced rapid aging, that his child would be hairless, stunted in growth, look like a little old man and die in his teens. Writing about this most unjust, most unacceptable death, Kushner addresses the question of losses and gains:

> "I am a more sensitive person, a more effective pastor, a more sympathetic counselor because of Aaron's life and death than I would ever have been without it. And I would give up all those gains in a second if I could have my son back. If I could choose, I would forgo all the spiritual growth and depth which has come my way because of our experiences, and be what I was fifteen years ago, an average rabbi, an indifferent counselor, helping some people and unable to help others, and the father of a bright, happy boy. But I cannot choose."

So perhaps the only choice we have is to choose what to do with our dead: to die when they die? To live crippled, or to forge new adaptations out of pain and memory? Through mourning we acknowledge that pain, feel that pain, and live past it. Through mourning we let the dead go. Through mourning we come to accept the difficult changes that loss must bring, and then we begin to come to the end of mourning.

Normally, we are not thinking of the negative possibilities, and we should not dwell on them, only recognize that they are there. We take our chances, and most of the time we win. We have many satisfactions and bundles of beautiful memories. That is the way life is put together, and we cannot change it. We deal with options, alternatives, and choices. **We cannot choose the direction or intensity of the wind, but we can adjust the sail.**

Grieving people are often told by well-meaning friends, "You just have to accept it!" That may be true, but it's not as easy as that, because it must be a decision of the heart; it must come from within. As we consider their advice, we need to know what they mean by the word "accept." Just ask them what they think it means.

Definition

Webster's New Collegiate Dictionary lists the following definitions of the word "accept."

1. "To receive with consent." No one would ever think of this meaning in relating to the loss of a spouse or child unless that person might have lived a hundred years and had been completely helpless for the last ten.

2. "To give admittance or approval to." We may admit or acknowledge it, but we have no inclination to approve it at this point.
3. "To endure without protest." No way!
4. "To regard as proper, normal, and inevitable." This would probably fit if the death had come in old age or after a lengthy illness.
5. "To receive as true—to understand." I don't like it and I don't agree with it, but I do understand it.
6. "To make a favorable response to." Hardly.
7. "To undertake the responsibility of." This has more to do with a business proposition or assignment.

Words mean what we intend them to mean. It is very possible that not a single one of the above definitions actually fits the way you feel about your loss right now, but you have the right to know what someone means when they tell you that you just have to accept it.

Don't be too concerned about your inability to accept your loss. Keep on doing your grief work, and someday you may discover that you are no longer concerned about accepting the loss. This means you are making progress.

There is an old story of an oak tree and a reed which grew close to each other on the side of a hill. One day the wind came with hurricane force, threatening to destroy them both. The oak stiffened its branches and prepared to fight, but the reed did nothing. After the storm had passed, the oak lay uprooted on its side while the reed, uninjured, soon stood as straight and tall as ever. When the dying oak asked the reed what made the difference, the reed replied: "I bent with the wind: I accepted it."

The Will to Recover

Author Judy Tatelbaum makes the striking statement in *You Don't Have to Suffer:* "Grieving is inevitable; recovering is not." It is a true statement, because not everyone who loses a loved one by either death or divorce does recover.

This does not include you, because you have been motivated to read this book as part of an effort to help yourself, and if you continue in your search for help, you will recover.

Sometimes during a serious illness, when a patient has reached a crisis, a member of the family might ask the doctor, "Is he going to get well?" The doctor may respond with something like "Much of it will depend upon the patient. We will do all that we can, and if he has a sufficient will to live, he can make it." We need to have the will to recover, and sometimes this amounts to a conscious decision to make a real effort to recover.

Mary had lost her husband in July, and she joined our grief group in November. She shared with us: "One day I just made up my mind. My husband is dead, but I am alive; he is gone, but I am here. So I'm going to get on with my life." And that's exactly what she did, and she did it well. Following such a decision, we just go on and do the things which will facilitate recovery. But unfortunately, sometimes the suffering following a sudden loss is so great and overwhelming that the survivor feels that life simply cannot go on. Writer Ann Kaiser Stearns provides this encouragement in *Living Through Personal Crisis:* "Certain circumstances are so overwhelmingly difficult that the best we can do to promote our eventual healing is simply to mark time, stay alive, and bear up under the worst of our suffering." Most anyone can do this, although it is not easy.

Recently, a very young widow whose husband died at the age of 30 and left her with a small daughter said in one of our groups: "I don't want to live any more." She said it with such sincerity and earnestness that all of us had fears of what she might do. That was more than a year ago. She somehow discovered that life could go on. Today, she has a good job and takes care of her daughter.

Turn to Chapter 2, *The Mourner's Path to Healing,* and follow the path down the left side of page 7 and beyond the LOWEST or TURNING point to the bottom of the page. This is where the path leads for someone who does not decide to work their way through to recovery, acceptance, and readjustment; resigning yourself to "poor me"; chronic depression; anger toward self and others; physical, mental and emotional illness; low life satisfaction; unhappiness, and NO REAL RECOVERY! That's about as desolate as the Dead Sea, and no one needs to go that way. Unfortunately, there are some people who will not avail themselves of whatever help might come from friends, family, faith, books, counselors, or a support group. All of us know people who have chosen this route, and they are dreadfully miserable.

Go On?

Shortly after the force of your loss has hit you, it is not unthinkable for you to feel that your life cannot go on. I think that most people who have lost their mate have felt this way at one time or another. If you have enough friends around you who minister to you and push away some of the clouds of grief and depression so you get to see the sun a little bit once in a while, your life can go on.

Unfortunately, there are some people who just don't want to go on, and no one can help them change their mind.

There are some problems in life for which there are no perfect solutions. Having to wear dentures is one of them, but millions of people have learned how to live with them. Some people are less able to accept them. I know a dentist who relates that he made three sets of dentures for a middle-aged lady. They didn't fit; they were too small; they were too big; they didn't feel right; when she wore them it felt like her whole head was full of teeth. She just would not accept them. She refused to wear them. She went on gumming her food for the rest of her life.

Many of us had a similar problem when we found out we had to wear eyeglasses, then bifocals or even trifocals. Most people get used to modifications like that with very little difficulty.

It does no good to fight the loss of a loved one. When we learn to live with the loss, we will have accepted it. Unfortunately, there are some people who simply refuse to accept what life hands them, and they are in perpetual crisis. It is not what happens to you that makes or breaks you, but what you do with it. When life hands you something you don't like and don't want to accept, you can do one of two things: forget it and run, or face it and recover. Blessed are the people like the legendary unsinkable Molly Brown—they can and will fight their way through anything, and that's impressive.

A number of years ago, a newspaper reporter interviewed a famous actress. Actors in the film industry are often looked upon to be very wise and real authorities on most anything. When he asked her, "What do you think of the universe?" she replied: "I accept it." Later in the day, he shared his experience with his cronies in the newsroom. When he told them about her answer to the universe question, one of the reporters remarked, "Gad, she might as well." Isn't that the truth?

Not infrequently we hear someone tell of a person who is suffering from a long, lingering and debilitating illness. They report, "He is at peace with his illness." In other words, he isn't fighting it. All of us have a great admiration for people in such a situation who can say, "If this is the way it is, this is the way it is."

Do you remember that Job, in the Old Testament, after all the bad things had happened to him, testified: "Though He slay me, yet will I trust Him (13:15)." This is faith in long trousers.

Refusing

You can't do anything constructive about trouble by refusing to accept it or by trying to run away from it. **<u>Non-acceptance does not change the fact.</u>** When someone comes to your door to deliver a message, you might do one of several things in response: shut the door in the face of the messenger; refuse to accept the message; or accept the message.

Most of us are familiar with Judge Wapner's "People's Court" on television. In one episode, a female tenant was hauled into court for non-payment of rent. The landlord had sent a representative of the marshal's office to the lady's apartment four times. All four times she had slammed the door in his face. When the judge asked her why she had done this, she replied: "I knew it was bad news." The judge laughed so hilariously that I thought he might fall out of his seat. He ruled against her. The fact that she refused to accept the message did not change the message or make it go away. Non-acceptance does not change the facts.

Arthur Freese in *Help for Your Grief* advises: "If we fail to accept death realistically, we will also fail in handling it intelligently and creatively. Only when we accept the reality of our loss can we go on and build."

There are several other typical responses to the death of a loved one, and all of us have heard them from time to time: "It's just my luck; that's fate; the cards are stacked against me; I'm angry about the whole thing; I resent God's permitting this thing to happen; I'm just going to stay home and forget about it; what's the use—you just have to put up with it; when your time is up, it's up—you can't do anything about it." Even such stoical attitudes as the above might help some people deal with their loss.

It was William James, the noted psychologist, who said near the close of his life in 1910, "The greatest discovery of my generation is that human beings can alter the circumstances of their lives by altering their attitudes." We are responsible for our attitudes because they mirror our inner feelings. If life rubs your fur the wrong way, maybe you need to turn around. Change your attitude. During the last two generations, millions of Americans have changed their attitudes about many fundamental things: race, color, human rights, the environment, etc. If our attitude is wrong or unwholesome, we can change it, and we should.

Following the end of hostilities in the Pacific in World War II, Emperor Hirohito of Japan was reported to have said in an address to his people: "We must now accept the unacceptable and surmount the insurmountable." Both of these things appeared to be impossible. The

Japanese people are as proud as any people, but they proved to the world that it is possible to accept the unacceptable and to surmount the insurmountable. We had won the war; did they have a choice? It was a bitter pill, but they took it. And now the world marvels at how far they have come since then.

Earl Grollman states in *When a Loved One Has Died:* "What is and cannot be changed must be accepted, even though it may be the most difficult thing you have ever done. You must face reality. The denial of tragedy is not mental health; mental health is the recognition of pain and the attempt to deal with it and live with it. The funeral is over, the flowers have withered, now the loss becomes real—your loved one has died."

Dorothy Hsu knows the meaning of this experience; she tells us about it in her book *Mending:*

"Last summer I sat in this spot by the neighborhood pool, and I worried about my husband, home, sick in bed. I could barely interrupt my thoughts to watch the girls splashing, to listen to their babbling. Four weeks later I sat by this pool stunned, immobilized, gripped by the fact that he was gone...

"This summer, I sit here again watching my girls play, reading, writing notes, planning for school next fall. Only occasionally nursing a pang when a family walks by, or a memory floats through—that's adjustment—to be able to sit nonchalantly by the pool, to eat again, to laugh again without pretending, to drive eleven hours to Toronto, alone with the girls, without panicking, to read a book entitled, *Why Do Christians Suffer?,* and discover that I think of my feelings in the past tense, to finally, after twelve months, switch my rings from my left hand to the right, to accept at last the fact that I'm no longer married. If adjustment (or acceptance) is being able to live again, without being constantly reminded of his absence, then I guess you could say I've adjusted. But if adjustment means never remembering and never hurting, then I guess one could say I'll never adjust."

The question of whether we can truly accept the death of a loved one remains debatable. We are all different in that we do not respond to a given situation in the same way. During the grieving process, we might admit that it has happened, it is final, irreversible, and now life must be faced alone. This realization is a part of the process of acceptance, and it brings an end to the relentless questioning process. We no longer need to ask WHY? Now our question should be WHAT NEXT? In other words, you don't have to fight it. Your acceptance becomes the end of a relentless questioning process. Normally this emotional acceptance nearly always follows the intellectual acknowledging.

Writer Linda Alderman substantiates this in *Why Did Daddy Die?:* "I am not sure that acceptance can ever be total. The death of a parent or spouse or child is an experience that most of us must live with for the rest of our lives. We learn to deal with our grief as it reappears in later life, but we never completely get over our loss. But there is a certain peace in knowing that we have survived. This is the normal grieving process."

4

Overcoming Loneliness

The Problem

It is paradoxical that in our age of communication explosion there are so many lonely people. Loneliness is a top-ranking mental health problem for many people. It is the price we pay for loving. Kenneth Patchen, the poet, wrote: "Loneliness is a bad place, a terrible place, it is a kind of hell." This does not mean that if you are lonely some of the time you are mentally ill. Everyone is lonely at one time or another; that's a part of being human. Loneliness is no respecter of age, race, creed, or economic status. It may occur when we are alone or when we are in a crowd. When a certain set of circumstances arises in our lives, we may become lonely.

But for one who has lost a loved one, loneliness is probably the most prevalent and difficult of the negative emotions we have to deal with. It seems to be a pre-packaged ingredient of grief. It is the absence of a particular loved one that makes the loss so cruel and difficult to adjust to.

Take the widow, for example: She is reminded of it every time she cooks a meal and then sits down to eat it alone; every time she tidies up her house she realizes that probably no one will come in that day to notice; any time she is alone and wants to talk, she knows there is no one there to answer; whenever she makes a decision, she is alone; every time she attends any kind of social function she is alone.

Mother Teresa said in an interview: "One of the greatest diseases is to be nobody to anyone." Think of that—to be completely without any vital ties to anyone; that is the ultimate poverty. Loneliness is the most desolate word in the English language.

Basically, loneliness has to do with our associations with other people. No man is an island. We are gregarious creatures and we need each other. In Carson McCullers' stage play *The Member of the Wedding* there is a scene following a wedding ceremony in a church. During the reception, when a kindly senior lady was strolling alone down one of the halls of the church, she came up to a door which was slightly ajar. Inside she could hear the sobbing voice of a girl. She entered and there sitting in one corner of the room was a teenage girl crying as though her heart was breaking. The kind lady placed a hand on her shoulder and inquired: "What is the matter? Why are you crying? Is there something I can do to help?" The girl replied: "Nobody's WE includes me. Everybody ought to belong to a WE, but I'm not a part of anyone's WE." The emotion of love and the closeness of the wedding ceremony and the idea of commitment it spoke of brought all this home to her. There was no one in the world who was as close to her as the closeness she had witnessed. She was alone and unloved. She was feeling the pain of rejection. When you use the term WE, whom do you include? How many other people are included in your WE? This is the real basis of loneliness—not being closely connected with anyone else.

Author Jean Libman Block spoke to the "aloneness" of the widow in *Back in Circulation:* "The vast majority...carry their burden of loneliness silently, grudgingly, resignedly, outspokenly, rebelliously, destructively...for months, years, or even a lifetime."

But does it have to go on interminably? Is there something one can do about it? Can loneliness be cured? Yes, it can. Read on; there's good news ahead.

Ms. Block goes on to say that loneliness is a symptom rather than a disease—"it announces the inner craving for intimacy and closeness." It should be thought of as a hunger pang. As hunger signals the need for food, so "loneliness proclaims an equally basic need...for companionship and closeness."

Life is too short to eat alone, shop alone, vacation alone, or spend our days alone. In short, life is too short to spend it being lonely.

Inactivity

It is not necessary to succumb to loneliness. There are all kinds of ways to break out of it. Earlier in this book I said, "There is help for your grief—that's the good news; the bad news is that you have to help yourself." The same is true of loneliness. There is help, but you have to help yourself. It cannot be overcome by inactivity. Loneliness cannot be cured by just being with people, seeing a counselor, or talking on the phone.

All of us have families and friends who sometimes try to get us to do all kinds of things we may not really want to do, and many times we go along with them just because they want us to. They intrude into our lives by suggesting, "We are going out shopping this afternoon; or we're going out to dinner tonight; or we'll take a ride in the country"—the WE meaning you and they. Others may try to guide us in other ways directing us away from loneliness, but there are some things we need to learn how to figure out for ourselves.

It is said that Albert Einstein, the world-famous physicist, once confided to a friend: "It is strange to me to be so lonely when I am so universally known." We can deduce from that statement that the great doctor was more interested in the study of physics than he was in taking time to develop relationships with people. Building strong and lasting friendships takes time and effort.

Many years ago when sailing vessels plied the oceans and seas of the world, because they had no refrigeration facilities many people developed scurvy, the direct result of a lack of Vitamin C found in fresh vegetables and fruit. When you have to go through life and you lack the basic fellowship, loneliness is sure to develop. If something is lacking in your social diet, you have to do something about it. There are many things you can do.

Loneliness is curable. Instead of wallowing in self-pity, we need to do something constructive about it.

Good News

Gary Greenwald in *Breaking Out of Loneliness* makes this surprising announcement: "Everything we need to know to resolve loneliness and break out of it already exists within us." Each of us creates and sustains our own loneliness. When we feel lonely, we are usually convinced that our loneliness is unalterable, or can be resolved through a difficult process, or that there is something lacking in us; or we may feel that the lack is in the outside world and we can only wait and hope. There are pathways that lead out: A person may die of thirst in a desert while standing a few feet above an underground stream.

"We cannot nourish ourselves so long as we are unaware of our ability to do so. When people feel boxed in and trapped, it is because they are limited by their own beliefs and habitual ways of responding."

It's Up to Me

Dr. J. Bradley Hoskisson, a British philosopher and scientist, in his book *Loneliness—An Explanation—A Cure,* makes a pertinent point in saying that a "person is really saying, 'It is up to someone else.' Until a person has faced the fact that it is principally and initially up to him, things will remain as they are and there will be no respite for the anguish of the heart." In other words, "What's going to be is up to me."

Be Busy

Being busy as a principle is probably as old as loneliness itself, but being busy just for the sake of being busy is not enough. The most rewarding kind of busyness is in doing for others without the anticipation of remuneration or reward, like sharing experiences and hopefulness with someone else by inviting another lonely person to have a meal with you in your home. Forget about the elegance of the menu. Spaghetti is no less acceptable than steak. Hamburger or beef stroganoff or sweet and sour chicken may be more satisfying than pheasant under glass. And being a hostess is not a bad position to be in. You become important to someone.

The time and effort it takes to prepare a meal for someone will keep your mind off your own problems and help keep your thoughts on a positive track.

People

One of the best antidotes for loneliness is people. More often than not, chronically lonely people are self-focused; they see only themselves and their own needs. The telephone company is constantly telling us: "Reach out and touch someone." It is also true that if you don't reach out, you may never be touched. It may seem easier to crawl into your hole and let the rest of the world go by as you languish in self-pity which is one of the human emotions that pays no good dividends.

Joining

Author and psychologist Jean Block cautions that "joining is the most typical cure for loneliness. But beware of the inherent pitfalls...your sense of isolation may be multiplied a thousandfold if you discover yourself on the edge and not really part of a cohesive group...to be among people who barely recognize your presence, who pass you by with hardly a glance or a word may crush the little that is left in your spirit. You may withdraw yourself, too wounded to make another attempt at venturing forth."

The antithesis to loneliness is belonging. Get out and join the world again. Join a group where you will be missed when the roll is called. Most people are lonely because they build walls around themselves instead of bridges to others. Become a part of somebody else's "WE." You will bring an end to your loneliness when you achieve intimate communication with other human beings. What is needed is friendship. Go out and seek friendships. Waiting around for someone to become a friend is not a positive step.

A meaningful relationship with another person need not be close to begin with. It could be an office associate, a neighbor, almost anyone you know. You get into conversation, just everyday small talk about small things. Put your total attention into that conversation. Listen. Reach out with all your being to that other human being who possibly might be as lonely as you are. When you make contact with that person, you will find, miraculously, that you are no longer lonely.

Jean Block sums it up with this counsel: "If you will pour all your feeling and intent into reaching out to establish a true rapport with another person, not just inattentive chatter or casual exchange of amenities or mechanical inquiry into his well-being, but communication, responsiveness, attention to the strongest and deepest sense of the word, then you have discovered the antidote for loneliness. For other lonely souls—and the world is full of them today—will intuitively recognize the life-restoring gift of communication which you are ready to offer them. They will turn to you as a plant turns to the sun. You will be able to build bridges of friendship and affection with many people, men and women."

Community

When Louise Berkinow traveled across America talking particularly to lonely people and some who were not, she discovered a possible solution to loneliness. Writing in *U.S. News and World Report,* she called the solution "creating community." A community is a group of people who are together, either in location or interest. She said, "The least lonely people I have met had done this. They also have strong friendships." This kind of plan calls for action. It requires effort on your part. You have to reach out and touch people. God made us for intimacy and companionship with others, and if we haven't achieved this, we are going to feel empty inside.

Scott Campbell, in his book *Widower,* makes the statement: "Part of living in this world is a matter of searching after and finding ways of being connected." The best way to find friends is to be one. Seek out another person, someone whom you could care about and with whom you could have a meaningful relationship based on friendship and caring. And remember, everyone prefers the company of happy, hopeful, and positive people.

It takes effort to make oneself into an interesting person. If you do nothing to make and keep friends, they will drop you like pearls of a broken strand of beads. Most grown women will remember the Girl Scout chorus: "Make new friends, but keep the old; one is silver, and the other is gold." Don't let wood, hay, and stubble grow where friendships should grow. It takes work and effort to grow a crop like this. It takes "get up and go" to make loneliness get up and go.

Problem or Challenge?

Loneliness may be viewed as either a problem or a challenge. Some of the greatest school teachers I have known never looked upon any child in their class as a "problem," but rather as a challenge. There's a big difference. Thinking about a "problem" is negative. Thinking about a challenge is exciting as we try to figure out what we're going to do about it.

Thinking about a situation or a person as a problem implies that we are accepting it and will just have to suffer it out. A challenge, on the other hand, stirs us up inside, gets the adrenaline flowing, as we roll up our sleeves for action. Problem thinking is always negative. Challenge thinking gets us to saying, "What am I going to do about it?" A teacher who accepts a problem child as a challenge is saying, "What can I do about this child; how can I love this kid; how can I bring out the best in him or her? How can I inspire him or her? How can I give him or her enough tasks to keep him or her busy and in the class?

All teachers have had their share of problem children, but if they thought of them as problems, teaching would be a drag and they would have a rough time getting up every day and going off to class. When you accept something as a challenge, you assume there is something you can do about it.

Loneliness is not reserved for the elderly. There are probably more lonely people among adolescents and young adults than there are among seniors. More things are planned for and being done with senior adults today than in any other period of our history. There are senior centers which provide many activities and make cultural programs available. Long and short trips are offered. There is no reason why anyone needs to stay home and do nothing all the time.

Reasons Why

One of the reasons there are so many lonely people is that nearly three times as many people live alone today as did in 1940. Many young men and women purchase homes or rent apartments to get away from their parents, choosing to live alone. This was not the case 50 years ago. This might be due in part to the fact that the family unit is not as strong as it used to be. Many families seldom eat their meals together, losing the opportunity for talking and discussing. There may be not enough emphasis on getting out among others, particularly in sporting events where they can meet new friends and interact with others. Perhaps it is the result of a natural desire to become independent as young people mature and parents today are more inclined to go along with it.

Another thing which contributes to loneliness and lack of meaning is the depersonalization of the individual. Do you know what the number is which you must use as a part of identification every time you perform a major business transaction? It's your Social Security number, and virtually everyone has one. We are human beings and we don't like to be reduced to a number. When I want to do business, I want to talk with a person. We don't want to be left on our own. What percentage of purchases do you make within a week's time in stores where there is no one to wait upon you, to explain something, or show you where something is? We are left on our own and many of us don't like it. I have had personal experience in trying to get to talk on the telephone with a particular person at a major bank and spent at least ten minutes being shuttled from one recorded voice to another before I finally got to talk with an actual person. I didn't like that, and said so to my bank's manager. We find this depersonalization in too many places. Human beings should be treated as people.

It should also be said that <u>we can be lonely in a crowd.</u> We may be in the midst of a hundred people and because we don't know any of them intimately, we tend to feel disconnected from everyone.

Studies show that men get lonely like women do, but won't admit to it because it might suggest a chink in their macho image. Loneliness may also vary with the seasons of the year. Statistics show that there are more suicides in the U.S. during December than any other time of the year, possibly because this season most always has to do with the gatherings of families, and this is when the lonely person feels his loneliness most keenly. You cannot take the holidays off the calendar. Face it; take more charge of these times. Don't let them just happen with you ending up being the victim rather than the victor. Make some plans. The holiday will happen no matter what you do. You should try to make it easier for yourself.

Circumstances

Loneliness is not always caused by circumstances; sometimes it is the result of a state of mind into which a person has fallen and has never gotten out. Loneliness may become a way of life for those who live in the past. Some years ago Nicki Cruz wrote a small book on *How Not to Be Lonely.* In it he recounts a conversation between an apartment house manager and Mamie, a senior tenant of his building. She is putting things away in a dumpster and the conversation goes something like this:

Manager:	"Mamie, you look a little down today. What seems to be the matter?"
Mamie:	"Oh, I don't know. Nobody seems to like me. I don't have any friends—nothing to do. I'm old and all alone in my apartment. Even my children won't come to see me."
Manager:	"Have you ever thought about volunteer work, Mamie? There's so much opportunity to help others."
Mamie:	"No, I can't do anything. Besides, who would listen to me? Nobody talks to me. Nobody cares what I do."
Manager:	"But you know, Mamie, there are so many people in the world much worse off than you are. What about old people? You could read to them."
Mamie:	"Certainly not! I can't stand old people."
Manager:	"What about children, then? There are hundreds of neglected children who need love and attention."
Mamie:	"Children? Absolutely not! I don't like to be around children. They make me nervous."
Manager:	"You could get a volunteer job in a hospital, Mamie. I've talked to lots of women who do that, and they just love it."
Mamie:	"I've already told you I can't do anything."

| Manager: | *(weary by now and running out of suggestions)* "Why don't you go to college, Mamie? Lots of mature people are continuing their education and find new meaning to life." |
| Mamie: | "Naw, I don't want to waste my time." |

What's wrong with Mamie anyway? First of all, she is all wrapped up in herself; she doesn't seem to have any time in her life for anyone else, even her children. It is a known fact that anyone who is all wrapped up in himself or herself is apt to be a small package. Secondly, she has a negative approach to most everything—always looking for a reason why she should not try something. Normally, most of us would not choose such a person to be a companion or a close friend. Finally, she has low self-esteem. She can't do anything and it seems she is unwilling even to try. There are many Mamies in the world. Please, don't you be one. Be willing to try most anything that sounds reasonable and sane. And remember, a mistake is evidence that someone tried. Try to get your loneliness under control before it gets too big, but that will take effort on your part.

Try It

Do something for someone else. It is one of the most rewarding ways to fill up lonely hours and give you a sense of having done something for someone else.

Celeste was an 80-year-old deaconess in a church which I served. Her husband had recently passed away at the age of 95. Since his passing, she was lonely most of the time that she was alone in her home. Depression became an all too frequent companion in her life. Then one day at noon, having spent a very depressing morning, she decided that if she would do something for someone else it might help, so she spent the afternoon visiting friends and acquaintances who were patients in convalescent and board and care homes—not exactly the most cheerful places in any community.

When she returned home late in the afternoon, she could not believe the change that had come over her. She was literally on top of the world.

What had she done that brought about the change? She had talked with everyone she visited, had written letters for a few, read for a couple of them and promised to make telephone calls for another—nothing really noteworthy or remarkable. But what a change it made in her!

When we are occupied in helping others, we feel significant, alive and happy. When we are not helping others, we tend toward despondency, inertia, and at times to loneliness. "Dear Abby" once said: "Are you lonely? The way to have friends is to be one. If nobody calls you, pick up the phone and call somebody. Go out of your way to do something nice for someone. It's a sure cure for the blues."

Get a Pet

Pets have some of the very best qualities for a relationship. They are loyal, uncritical, non-judgmental, relatively undemanding, and they are usually there. A dog will often cry when you leave the house, and your neighbors will testify that it cries most of the time while you are away. When you come home, it jumps all over you and sometimes runs through all the rooms of the house to show how glad it is that you are home again. You just can't beat that for a relationship! A good pet offers companionship and comfort. A dog offers a feeling of safety and a reason to get out and exercise.

However, there are some disadvantages to owning a pet. You have to feed it, take it to the vet once in awhile, and find a place for it to stay when you are away for a few days. A pet can be a lot of work, but nurturing something other than yourself can contribute immeasurably to good mental health. A dog that barks when someone comes to the door provides valuable security. A cat is a great companion and can be as independent as its owner. Showing or breeding animals can bring rich rewards, often forming the basis for new friendships. Most pet owners would agree that the advantages far outweigh the disadvantages.

Researchers have found that women who owned dogs experienced less stress when their husbands died than women who did not have dogs. These women appeared better able to cope with the loss.

I know of a senior lady, long divorced, who was as kind and considerate a neighbor as anyone could ever wish for. Then one day something occurred in our park. The all-male tenants' committee had made a decision with which she disagreed, which turned her against every male in the place. She never had a word with any of them. If they were about to meet on the street, she would quickly dart to the other side and never even look up. What an ugly transformation! She seemed to be upset with everyone.

One of her neighbor ladies was having to give up her home and move into an apartment where she could not keep her little dog. Everyone was surprised when Mrs. Out of Sorts agreed to adopt the pooch. Then magical things happened in her home. After six months of caring for that little mutt, loving it and being loved by it, it had transformed her back into the lovable and caring neighbor she had been in the years before. A miracle performed by a little dog!

Just in case you need a little help in coming up with ideas of things you can do to combat loneliness, the following list should be helpful. I found some of them in Betty Jane Wylie's *Beginnings,* or the later edition which was titled *Survival Guide for Widows,* on page 102 of an excellent chapter on loneliness:

1. Make a list of the clothes you would like to get rid of and new ones you would like to purchase.
2. Paint a room or refinish some furniture.
3. Clean the oven—yuck!
4. Polish the silverware.
5. With everything clean, have a party!
6. Cook up a storm for that party.
7. Cook something you've never cooked before but always wanted to try.
8. Treat yourself to a new hairdo.
9. Get out of the house if you really don't have to be there.
10. Scream.
11. Pray.
12. Forgive someone.
13. Write something—letters, poems, a diary.
14. Take trips—short ones and some to far-away places which you have never seen.
15. Meaningfully occupy your time.
16. Set some goals for the next two months.
17. Look to the future without forgetting the past.
18. Every day take good care of yourself.
19. Purchase some new clothes.
20. Plan some dinner parties for others who also are lonely and whom you would like to know better.
21. Do some things you haven't done before, but really wanted to.
22. Enroll in a class to learn some new things or brush up on some old things.
23. Get into politics.
24. Come to the breakfast table dressed for the day.
25. Get into politics—support a worthwhile cause.
26. Attend community meetings, City Council, etc.
27. Adopt an exercise regimen: swim, jog, walk, bicycle.
28. Do something really nice for someone who deserves it.

29. Attend concerts, programs, etc.
30. Become a volunteer in a good cause which will outlive you.
31. Become a volunteer at your local hospital.
32. Learn to make things—join a craft group.
33. Take a class in something you have always wanted to know more about.
34. Learn to play golf or a musical instrument.
35. Go back to school and get the high school/college diploma you don't have.
36. Now that you have time, wake up a dream you had when you were younger, but it's been asleep on the shelf for years.
37. Force yourself to get out among the living.
38. Do accept invitations from your friends even though you may feel like a fifth wheel and you are afraid you might cry at an inappropriate time, or you don't like to dress up.
39. Take yourself in hand—refuse to isolate yourself.
40. Seek a new romantic relationship.
41. Establish a network of friends and activities to help you start a new life.
42. Practice the Golden Rule: Show as much concern toward others as you would want them to show to you.
43. Don't become so preoccupied with work and other things that you shut yourself off from your loved ones and friends.

Before loneliness can disappear from your life, you must take the first step—attune yourself to someone else by listening with not only your ears, but with your heart, your mind, your eyes, and even with your hands. There is magic and warmth in the human touch. Reach out and touch someone. When you give someone else your total attention, there will come back to you a healing and restorative balm to the arid places of your life.

Finally, it's also a good thing to keep records of when and under what circumstances loneliness hits you (weekends, Sunday afternoons, the time your loved one normally got home from work each day), and plan a strategy that will sidetrack loneliness and keep you on track in the right direction. And as Ms. Wylie said: "Go through with it. You have to, you know. There's no turning back."

Perseverance in the face of disappointment is essential in learning how to cope. It takes "get up and go" to make loneliness get up and go.

5

Handling the Holidays

Holidays get a bad rap from most grieving people. They are worse than Sundays or weekends. Non-grieving people look forward to holidays, anniversaries and other special days with excitement and keen anticipation. This is not true of the grieving, because when you laid your loved one into the arms of God, you became equipped with an automatic calendar inside you; when the anniversary month nears, no one needs to tell you that you are going to miss your loved one dreadfully, and it seems to you that you are heading for the pit of despondency and you cannot see how you are going to get through it. Death has forever changed the meaning of the holiday season for you. Your heart is filled with dread, fear, and sadness instead of joy, because these special days are associated with family togetherness. Now that a member of your family is no longer present, there will be memories of happier times together and sadness will take the place of joy. You don't make it happen; it just happens.

My use of the term "holiday" includes not only special family times like Thanksgiving, Christmas and Easter, but also anniversaries, birthdays, special memory days, weekends, and other dates which have been particularly dear to you. Meg Woods in *The Toughest Days of Grief* says: "No affection, no loyalty, no compassion, no tie is as strong and abiding with a living person as it is with a dead one." It was Henry Wadsworth Longfellow who said: "The holiest of all holidays are those kept by ourselves in silence and apart: the secret communications of the heart."

Be assured that all the apprehension you might have in facing a holiday season does not mean that you are abnormal; rather, you would be abnormal if it were otherwise. No matter how well you may have been getting along with your bereavement recovery for the past months, when you become aware of the coming of a holiday there will be some fear and dread, because your sorrow becomes vivid and sharply focused on memories of your loved one and the memorable ways you spent such times together, and you feel the freshness and hurt of your loss, particularly if your relationship with the lost one was very close. In their passing, a large part of you has been torn away; things are not the same and you are now living a strange, new role: You still live in the same house; it has the same furnishings; days still have 24 hours in them, but they seem like 48 hours because they pass so slowly. Your lot is now cast in a new world filled mostly with depression and sadness, and you feel that you can never be happy again.

It is true in this regard as well as in many other areas of life—if you are facing a difficult situation, like a holiday or memory day, if you will wisely plan for the day and carry through with your plans, you will discover that many of the clouds in your sky will dissipate and you will find some sunlight shining through, because you decided to face up to it and get through it the best way you could.

Studies made in this area of bereavement indicate that most people came to see that their dread of the holiday was much more difficult and threatening than the actual occurrence of the special day. Most people agree that after it was over, and if they really planned how they would get through it, it wasn't as bad as they thought it was going to be, and they wasted a lot of energy worrying about it. It can be that way with you. But it's up to you to do something to help defuse the situation. Good things do not just happen automatically; more often they are contrived. Don't knock it if you haven't tried it. Dr. Joyce Brothers in *Widowed* says: "We cannot turn them into happy occasions, but we can make them easier to live through." And that takes some planning. Nobody promises you that it's going to be a hilarious blast. There will be pain no matter what you do.

Beverly Gordon in her excellent book *The First Year Alone* tells her own experience: "A year ago, I was grieving the loss of my mother, and the holiday season held no joy for me. People told me that the first Christmas without her would be the hardest and that I would feel differently in the future, but I did not believe them. I was sure that the Christmas spirit had left me forever. This year, however, I have been surprised to find it filling me again."

In this chapter, I will be sharing with you some suggestions about options and alternatives which I hope you will be courageous enough to try to incorporate into your life. What I will be saying does not amount to the last word on the subject. There is no right way to grieve in five easy steps, and there are no magic pills to take. Every grief is unique, and we are all different. What works for one person may not do for another.

"Different strokes for different folks." Experiment should be the road we take.

Make certain to keep telling yourself that you cannot bring back the old, but with some planning and doing you can celebrate the new. What you make out of the ashes of your grief is up to you. Try counting your blessings instead of your burdens. You cannot deny the existence of the special day, but you can commit yourself to deal with it constructively. Remember the past and the happy occasions; they are important; also turn your face and plans to the future. Just as there was a past, there will also be a future. "This too shall pass away."

The prospect of a holiday can look like an insurmountable obstacle along the road ahead. Here are your options: Try to forget it and run, or face it and win. Take charge of what happens and don't just let it happen, with you becoming the victim of the circumstance. No matter what you do, the whole experience may be bittersweet. There will be sadness, depression, and maybe even wishing you were dead. Holidays are meant to be happy, so don't let your grief and loneliness get the upper hand. If you are planning to stay at home over the holidays, alter your plan and don't stay alone. To cite Joyce Brothers again, she mentioned in her book how she dreaded the first Thanksgiving after her husband's death. She decided to entertain all 18 members of her family at their farmhouse. Being a hostess is not a bad position to be in.

If you don't have family near, surely you know some people who also will be alone on the holiday. Why not invite several to share the day with you? You might even make it a potluck arrangement.

Don't turn down invitations from friends because you are afraid of being a fifth wheel, or you are afraid you will cry at an inappropriate time, or you don't like to dress up. Refuse to isolate yourself. Force yourself to be out among the living.

Just Another Day?

I have heard people say that they just won't think of it as a special day. "I'll just regard it as another day." You are going to have a problem with that one, because it's *not* going to be just another day, and you know it. When you start kidding yourself about something like this, your mind is playing tricks on you which might result in trouble. This is denial. There is nothing you can do about anything as unalterable as a date on the calendar. You could even tear all twelve months from it, but your feelings about your loss would not have changed. Time does not stop. It does no good to deny what has happened; it's much better to deal constructively with it.

I believe that loved ones should be remembered and even talked about at holiday occasions, but not the way Mrs. Going did. She and her husband had lost a son several years before and she related to a friend how awful the holidays were. It seemed they spent most of the day talking about him, especially at mealtimes. She indicated that "before the meal was over, everyone was in tears. It was just like having the funeral all over again," and this had been going on for several years. This is one way not to remember at holiday time. If there needs to be talk about the loved one, and there should be, the conversation should be about funny things the loved one did, or said; some special reasons why you remember him; something that makes you laugh; some mistakes he made. Be upbeat and creative. Each person around the table might be asked to write a note of remembrance and read it after the meal.

I think the empty chair and place setting at the table is all too obvious and negative in its effect. Why not just have one lighted candle on the table and everyone knows it's there in the loved one's memory? A candle suggests light, warmth, and coziness. Isn't that what our loved one gave us? Some families take gifts of food, clothing or toys to charities on particular days, such as a birthday or a holiday. Make sure you deliver them in person, and not just write a check to the Salvation Army or some other agency. Give the children in the family a share in planning how they want to remember their sibling. And don't forget the loved ones you still have during the holidays—or any other time! You can control more things than you think you can, but it's up to you.

Cope

The first letters of the first words in the following section form an acrostic, COPE, which means "to fight off; contend with; to deal creatively and constructively with." I arranged it this way to make it easier to remember. These are all strong action words; they have to do with *doing* something. You are not defending yourself; you are initiating that battle; you are on the offense and you are out to win. Anyone can do this—you don't have to be Superman or Superwoman. The words are not listed in the order of importance, it's just that "cope" must be spelled this way; but each one can be helpful. Try them. Something good might happen.

1. **Change location,** occupy another place; vacate the premises; put yourself in other surroundings. Did you notice I said "put yourself"—

you have to do it. For many people at holiday times this is an option or an alternative. If you can, go somewhere; be in some other place.

Fundamentally, I do not recommend running away, but in warfare there are times when a fighting unit must pull back, retreat, rest awhile, regroup and then go back into the fray. If you have always celebrated Thanksgiving and/or Christmas with relatives and close friends in your own home, why not try to be away over the holiday, but not necessarily alone. Many widows and widowers feel that their children might be inviting them to spend the holiday with them out of a sense of pity. Within himself a widower might ask: "Are they doing this out of pity, or just because they don't want me to be alone?" Sam, a widower in one of my Bereavement Recovery Groups, said in a meeting a few years ago: "I felt this way when my children asked me to their home for Thanksgiving dinner. But I had another idea; there was something else I would rather be doing, so I told them: 'You know, I have this friend in Golden, Colorado. We've been writing to each other for years, and he's always asking me to come and visit him, as he, too, had lost his wife. Finally, I'm going to see Joe and see if I can't cheer him up a bit over the holidays. I hope you won't mind. I'll be okay. But I'll come back and then maybe we can share Christmas together.'" They gave him their blessing, and he had a wonderful time, because he had asked himself the question, "What really do I want to do during this holiday season?"

This sort of plan has to do with mind control. While we are with others who were not a part of our previous celebrations, we are constantly thinking of them; we listen to their conversation and we respond. Or if we're on a trip or a cruise, we're doing all sorts of new things, meeting new people, seeing things new to us. As a result, most of the time our minds are momentarily being relieved of painful memories. There is an old saying which goes like this: "You cannot prevent the crows from flying around in the air, but you can prevent them from building a nest in your hair." We can control the directions of our thoughts more than we do—but WE have to do it. The Apostle Paul believed in mind control and suggested that Christians practice it. In Philippians 4:8, he says: "Whatsoever things are true, honest, just, pure, lovely [etc.], think on these things." Being in another place, amidst new or different surroundings, with other people, will help you think about the right things. The presence of others will keep you from thinking about the lost loved one, or indulging in self-pity.

What I have just said about holidays applies also to other days. Get out of your house as often as you can. You already know about how the walls begin to close in on you; you don't always have to be at home; there are so many interesting places to go, people to see and new things to do, but you have to take the initiative; you have to do it yourself. You are fortunate if you have at least one friend who constantly encourages you to do this and may even offer to accompany you. You need to be in charge of your own life and plans. Decide what you can be comfortable with and share this with your family.

Sometimes in warfare a portion of the fighting force will retreat for awhile, not because they are losing or giving up, but they are tired and need to work out some new strategies. Having done this, they go back into the fray to win. When we are away, we are better able to see things in their proper perspective and will be better able to deal with them.

For most of us there are almost always options or alternatives. In your grief, do you ever feel that you are like the captive steer being driven up a cattle chute, with a six-foot wall on both sides? The path is too narrow to run around in and change course, and someone is behind you pushing you on with a prod or a whip. The feeling may be natural and normal, but that's really not your situation. You can be in control of your life and direct your own course if you really want to. You can do more than you think you can—try it! You might be in for a surprise.

My friend Norma is a case in point. She's one widow I know who does almost everything right. Within a year she lost both her husband and her only child, a daughter of 43 years who had never presented her with a grandchild. Those are sizable losses, but she has learned to cope well with them. For many years she has been seriously involved as a volunteer in our local hospital. A big chunk of most of her days is spent doing this kind of volunteer work.

One Friday afternoon at about 5 o'clock, she drove her car onto her driveway, turned the engine off, and sat for a few moments. Seemingly from nowhere came the thought: "What a horrible weekend this is going to be, with me alone and nothing I really have to be doing." This kind of depressive thinking can occur any time and anywhere, and without notice. But Norma got her options-alternatives machine to functioning. As soon as she got inside the house, she called a dear lady friend in Sacramento, about 60 miles away. "What are you doing this weekend?" she inquired. "Nothing in particular," said the friend. "Would you like to come up?" "I certainly would." And within less than half an hour she had farmed her little dog out to her neighbor and was on her way to Sacramento. About 5 o'clock Sunday afternoon, she again parked her car on the driveway and said to herself: "What a terrific weekend this has been; we went to lunch together, we shopped in the mall, we went out to dinner together, we talked up a storm almost every waking hour we were together. I'm surely glad I didn't stay home." This lady is really in charge of her life. She did not want to accept "What a horrible weekend this is going to be." She did something that changed it.

The next time you're in such a situation, take a little time to survey the alternatives: "Where would I rather be; what would I rather be doing; with whom would I like to be?" Your world is full of options and alternatives, but you have to find them and act on them.

2. **Others:** One of the most therapeutic things you can do during the holiday season, or any other season, is to do something for someone else. There is no more effective way of fighting depression or the blues than to give of yourself in helping another. Here is a law of life which I hope you will memorize: **Anyone who helps another out of a hole (trouble, distress, loss, disappointment, loneliness, or whatever) will, without even trying, lose some of his own burdens and problems in that hole; this is a miracle. Some miracles only God can bring about; this is one which he has reserved for you to perform.**

Happiness is contagious; if you try to make others happy, you can hardly avoid catching some of it yourself. In loving you will be loved. Reach out instead of wallowing in self-pity, and while you are helping another, your mind will not be dwelling on your own loss and the resulting sorrow.

The Christmas holidays are times of special loneliness for many people; that is probably the reason why the incidence of suicide is greater then than at any other period of the year. If you have no family to share a holiday with, why not reach out and touch someone else? Invite them to your home. Share a well-planned and prepared meal with one or more friends. Take the initiative. Amy Ross in *By Death or Divorce* learned that three persons at her workplace would be alone over a holiday. She invited all of them to her house. She makes the statement: "You will never feel like an outsider in your own home. Nor will you need to worry that you have been included (at someone else's home) out of pity. Being host or hostess, for awhile at least, is a nice position to hold." If you're not up to bearing the whole load, make it a shared (potluck) meal.

Beverly Gordon in *The First Year Alone* tells of her own experience. "I have made up my mind not to accept any Thanksgiving or Christmas invitations. I know there are those who will press me to change my mind, but I have to make them understand that I need to trust my own feelings on matters like this, to listen to my inner self. I would rather stay home in familiar, comfortable surroundings this year, so when I discovered that Mary would be alone at Thanksgiving and that Debbie is not going home for Christmas, I invited them to share those holidays with me. **If I had** to sum up the solution to handling the holidays in one phrase, it would have to be: Force your thoughts to reach out to others, instead of allowing them to be directed inward to self-pity."

3. **Plan ahead:** Prior to 1976, the typical 7-Eleven convenience store was held up at gunpoint at least once a month. Of the 7,500 stores, the cash losses averaged $3,000 per store per year. Now that has all changed. Despite a 74 percent increase in retail robberies nationwide from 1976 through 1982, now the typical 7-Eleven is robbed less than once every 30 months and cash losses have fallen to a mere $38 per store per year. What made the difference?

They hired Ray Johnson, a former armed robber, through the Western Behavioral Science Institute in La Jolla, California. He recommended simple, inexpensive site modifications. First of all, they reduced window advertising to a minimum and installed exterior lighting. The cash register was moved up front and placed low enough for a customer to see for himself that it contains very little money—usually less than $30. Back door and alley exits were eliminated. A Time Access Cash Controller (floor safe) was installed. If a clerk needs more money to complete a transaction it would take two minutes for the safe to open. Placards in the store tell the customers that. With such safeguards, only a fool would be crazy enough to risk a jail sentence with the cards so stacked against his success. The whole possibility has been defused.

What does this all mean? If you plan ahead for what might be coming, it might not come, or if it does, its impact will be less than if you had not planned.

In areas of the world frequented by hurricanes and tornadoes, as soon as the storm watch is sounded over radio or TV and it is determined that it will be a severe storm, what do you think people in the area will be doing before the storm reaches them? They will be nailing sheets of plywood over large windows, things that are loose will be put under shelter or tied down, and people will be seeking a safe shelter. This calls for action—not just reaction.

4. **Execute your plans:** Good intentions and plans have no value unless they are expedited and carried through. After you have decided what you really want to do during the holiday and what you would feel comfortable with—follow through. I think there sometimes is a real danger in trying to do what you think your loved one would do. You are now in charge and need to make your own decisions. You cannot change the past, but you need to take care of the present.

Charles lost his wife in July, and he had no family but a brother and his wife who had two small children. Out of concern for the bereaved brother, he was invited to spend Christmas day with their family, as they lived in the same city. He responded by saying, "I will come over Christmas morning and have breakfast with your family and will stay until everyone has opened the presents from under the tree. Then I will go home and return at 2 o'clock and share dinner with you; the rest of the day I will spend in my own home." You see, he knew what he wanted to do, what plan of action would best suit his needs. Everything went as planned. Afterward he related: "After I came home following breakfast, I turr.ed on the stereo and played beautiful music all morning, while I read a book, did some remembering of better days, counting the blessings rather than the burdens. I also cried a little. After dinner, I continued with the same things. As I look back over the events of the day, I'm satisfied that I spent it in the way that was best for me." Time spent alone can be very rewarding. Solitude is a good place to be sometimes, but it's no place to live.

In a recent column of Dear Abby, she quotes a letter from an aging grandmother who really knew her own mind: "My daughter and her family think I am the worst kind of monster because I refuse to travel 500 miles to spend the holidays with them in complete clutter and turmoil. Their home is a zoo at holiday time, with dozens of people coming and going and so much noise from music and shouting; it takes me a month to recover when I return. I am 79 and enjoy being home. Thank you. Party Pooper in Alabama." Keeping afloat is largely a matter of navigating.

In 1987 Ann Landers published her *Coping with Grief During the Holidays* in one of her daily columns. The first nine suggestions following are hers and relate principally to holidays such as Christmas, Thanksgiving, etc.; the remainder are from other sources, like pebbles I picked up on the seashore but don't remember exactly where:

CHANGE TRADITIONS. Have Christmas dinner at a different house this year. It is a paradox that the more you try to make it the same as it was before, the more obvious your loved one's absence will be.

BALANCE SOLITUDE WITH SOCIABILITY. Solitude can renew strength. Being with people you care about can be equally important. Plan to attend some holiday parties. You may surprise yourself by having a good time.

RELIVE THE HAPPY MEMORIES. Pick three special memories of past holidays with your loved one. Recall them often, especially if outbursts of grief seem to occur at an inappropriate time.

SET ASIDE "LETTING GO" TIME. Schedule specific time on your calendar to grieve. When you know you set aside this time, it will be easier for you to postpone your flow of grief in public.

COUNTER THE CONSPIRACY OF SILENCE. Because family and friends love you, they may think they are doing you a favor by not mentioning your loved one for fear you will be upset. Break the ice by mentioning him or her yourself. Tell your family and friends that it is important for you to talk about your loved one during the holiday season when that missing person is very much on your mind.

FIND A CREATIVE OUTLET. Write a memorial poem or story about your loved one and share it. Contribute to or work with a group that your loved one supported. Use the money that you would have spent for a gift for that special person to buy something for someone he or she cared about.

DON'T FORGET THE REST OF THE FAMILY. Try especially hard to make it a good holiday for the children. Listen to them. Talk to them. If decorating the tree or buying Christmas gifts is too difficult for you to do this year, ask a friend to do it for you.

UTILIZE AVAILABLE RESOURCES. If your faith is important to you, participate in the holiday church services. Some veterans of the faith have a serenity, a kind of healing wisdom. They can help you. Seek out a support group of other grieving people. Or start your own short-term support group to help you through the holidays.

ABOVE ALL, REMEMBER that you cannot change the past, but you can take care of the present. Total recovery might never come, but what you kindle from the ashes of your tragedy is largely up to you.

VISIT RELATIVES or choose friends with whom you are comfortable.

CLEAR YOUR MIND—admit your painful feelings.

PARE DOWN some "trimmings" so you can relax and enjoy others' company.

GO TO A RESORT alone or with a close friend.

DO SOMETHING FOR SOMEONE ELSE:
  Send a meal you prepared.
  Offer to drive someone on errands.
  Take care of a busy mother's children.
  Take some otherwise homebound person shopping with you.
  Call someone who is alone.

Bake cookies, especially for and with children.

Invite someone to lunch or dinner and say, "I'll come and get you and take you home."

If you have a widow friend who is harried, overworked, and overwrought with so many responsibilities that she can't seem to get with keeping her house clean, show up at her place some morning, loaded with cleaning materials and equipment, and announce: "I am an angel from heaven. I do windows, floors and anything else your house might need. My commission says I am yours today; where do you want me to start?" After you've fallen into each other's arms and laughed and cried a bit and had a cup of coffee together, you will find it will be a great day for both of you.

STOP YOURSELF from thinking bad and sad thoughts.

TRY NOT TO "awfulize" the holiday.

CELEBRATE THE SEASON, but don't forget the reason.

IF MEMBERS OF YOUR FAMILY or friends are going to share a meal together, and if they feel it would be appropriate and healing, those who wish to do so might write a note of remembrance—something the absent loved one said or did; something funny you remember about them; your appreciation for the way they lived their life. Notes may be placed together and each one reads one—they may be signed or unsigned.

GO FOR A WALK alone or with a close friend.

CHOOSE THE RIGHT people you would want to be with on the holidays—those who allow you to share your honest feelings and accept you for what you are.

IT IS HARD for you to imagine that anyone else could be more miserable than you are. During the year that ended today, 500,000 women in America became widows; millions of parents are grieving the loss of a child; others' lives are devastated because of a divorce. They have needs that you can address—freely give food, clothing, fellowship, and understanding.

HAVE A FAMILY COUNCIL to decide what the holiday will consist of.

START A NEW TRADITION—include something you haven't included before.

DON'T DUMP THE "good" of an old tradition.

DRESS YOURSELF UP and take yourself out.

PURCHASE AN EXPENSIVE GIFT for yourself and wrap it as you would if you were giving it to someone else.

IF YOUR EATING HABITS ARE BAD and you don't know what to cook, carefully walk through the delicatessen at your favorite supermarket. You might even purchase some items to take home.

SEND A LIVING PLANT to a grieving friend's home—let them know you are thinking of them.

INSTEAD of working overtime to buy a present for your youngster, spend more time with that youngster.

WHAT WOULD YOU want to be feeling or thinking if you were to enjoy the holiday?

BE ASSERTIVE—your friends and loved ones need to know that you are in charge of your life.

THINK STRAIGHT and keep your expectations reasonable.

DON'T PERMIT your loved ones or friends to level a guilt trip on you when you don't want to do what they think you should do.

CONTRIBUTE TO or work for a group your loved one supported.

SORT OUT YOUR FEELINGS—what would make the holiday meaningful for you?

WHAT WOULD you really like to do? Try to arrange it.

MAKE PLANS, then execute them. Think through them often so you become comfortable with them—if you don't feel comfortable with them, they should be altered.

COMMUNICATE with a longtime friend from whom you have heard nothing for months. "Reach out and touch someone."

BE POSITIVE—keep telling yourself, "I will survive this holiday" and you will. Believe in yourself.

TAKE TIME to be nice to yourself.

DECIDE that sometime in the next two or three years you will organize the holiday festivities and have everyone at your place.

VOLUNTEER to help serve meals at the local mission, or accompany your church or association when they visit hospital and nursing homes. It will make you feel needed.

DO NOTHING SPECIAL; be a free spirit for a few hours or days. After all, you are not obligated to spend all your time contributing to the gross national product.

TRY TO ACCEPT the fact that you will find yourself going through the motions without the customary emotions.

AVOID TRYING to make it like it was before, because if you do, the more obvious your loved one's absence will be.

IF YOU ARE THINKING that the Thanksgiving holiday is a cruel joke, pray this prayer:

I'm thankful, Lord, for loving care;
I'm thankful, too, for something more;
I'm thankful, Lord, that I can bear
Some things I'm really not thankful for.

Some of the things I have mentioned may not be for you; keep searching and surveying the options and alternatives until you find the things that would help you. Total recovery will never come for you; you will never get over your grief, but you can GET THROUGH IT.

When the sun sets on the holiday, no matter what happened to you, you will have survived and you are now one day nearer whatever recovery you make for yourself.

You should know that your pathway is filled with dangerous land mines—moments of painful realization of your loss and resentment toward a world that seems to go on without noticing or caring.

Meg Woodson has written a whole book on this subject, *The Toughest Days of Grief*. It was published by Zondervan in 1994. If you need more ideas, she has dozens of them. Your local library has a copy or can secure one for you.

6

Grief Work: The Things We Do That Help Us Through*

The Tasks of Mourning

In *The Courage to Grieve,* Judy Tatelbaum makes the statement: **"The most basic cause of unsuccessful grieving is our lack of knowledge about experiencing and completing the mourning process."** The things which are a part of successful grieving are good things for you to know right now. Making your way through grief is somewhat like navigating a sailboat, facing contrary winds. **Just remember: you cannot control the direction or velocity of the wind, but you can adjust the sail.**

The Task

You have been deprived, by death or divorce, of the love and companionship of someone closely entwined with your life. This is called bereavement—you are bereft of a loved one. The dreams and hopes you shared as a couple are now only memories. Something terrible has happened. Your life will never be the same again. This fact can never be changed; it is irreversible. Everything you do about your loss in an attempt to reorganize so you can go on with your life is called "grief work." Sigmund Freud was probably the first person to use this phrase. It means just what it says—the tasks of mourning, the work we have to do to get through the experience of mourning. This will probably be the most difficult and challenging work assignment of your life.

To consider an analogy might be helpful at this point. Let us suppose that you live in a mobile home, and it is situated in earthquake country.

*Some portions of this section have been adapted from the author's ***The Mourning After.***

You are aware that if a real shaker comes along, the pillars which hold your house up could be dislodged and your home could end up lying flat on the ground. What a mess! When the shaking stops, you come back into the house and survey the situation: So much of your beautiful and expensive glassware, etc., would be lying broken on the floor. If you are a normal woman, probably your first impulse will be to break out in tears. If you are a man, you will probably use some unparliamentary words, and you might as well, because the carnage will seem complete and unfixable. After the crying and naughty words are over, what will you do next? Clean up the mess. The items which are broken beyond repair are consigned to the trash bucket. Those which are still usable you put back where they belong. You go on doing this, little by little, until finally your house is somewhat put back together again, minus things you will miss for a long time. Grief does not go away by itself, like your house, which will not put itself together; you have to work at it.

The very same things you do in putting your house back together after an earthquake are the kinds of things you do after you lose a loved one. Everything you do that is aimed at getting your life back on track can probably be called "grief work." It is work, hard, long, painful, slow, repetitive, as you suffer through the same effort over and over again. A matter of rethinking, refeeling, reworking the same old emotional field, breaking through the denial and disbelief, until finally the past, like the deceased, is ready to be buried. Out of all this, a stronger you emerges with the attitudes, concepts, values, and appreciation of life itself. If some of these are better than the old ones, then there has been growth and change.

Getting Through

You may never get over your grief, but you can get through it. People who do not do their grief work are the ones who after three or four years cannot speak about their loss without breaking into tears. You shouldn't have to do this after that many years.

Attending a support group, reading books, or attending lectures about grief management, or having a close friend as a mentor—these are some of the ways that can help you to get both feet somewhat on the ground. You will make a little progress and slowly get on with your life, even though the memory of your loss will always be with you. Recovery doesn't happen overnight. Sometimes the progress seems so slight that it's imperceptible. But then, how does one move a mountain? Whether you use high-powered, heavy equipment, or a hand shovel, it's still one shovelful at a time.

Sometimes the progress is so slow that you become discouraged and feel that you just aren't getting anywhere. In *Grieving,* Therese Rando has an excellent chapter on "What Recovery Will or Will Not Mean." Please get this book and read it over and over again until the content is firmly imbedded in your mind.

Out of the Ashes

On November 28, 1942, 492 people lost their lives in the Cocoanut Grove nightclub fire in Boston. Following this dreadful disaster, Dr. Eric Lindeman, a psychologist associated with Massachusetts General Hospital, decided to do something to help the hundreds of survivors of this tragedy. He enlisted the aid of dozens of psychologists, psychiatrists, and counselors who worked with them over a period of two years. In his paper reporting on the results of this effort, *The Symptomatology and Management of Acute Grief,* he defines grief work as the "tasks and processes you must complete successfully in order to resolve your grief." It's very much like a road map which tells you how to get to a certain destination. Another author defines it as a "process of working out and living through some painful feelings, coming to some tough decisions, and performing some difficult actions." It's all the things we do that help us through. Lindeman sums it up in these words: "The healing depends on how well the person does the grief work," plus the length and quality of the relationship. It's all the things we do that help us through. It's painful, but it pays; it hurts, but it works.

How long does the grieving process take? You will notice on the *Path* chart in Chapter 2, at the top of the right-hand column: "Readjustment, resolution, acceptance, recovery—one or two years from the time of loss is normal." This could even be stretched to four or five years, because not everyone progresses at the same speed. Grief is a terrible emotional wound which does not heal quickly.

Pain

Therapy is always painful. Just imagine yourself in a hospital bed; you had abdominal surgery from top to bottom the day before, and you're staring up at the ceiling; every nerve in your body is registering pain and hurting so badly that you could not imagine anyone ever pulling through a thing like this. Then some sweet little thing, all dressed in white, flits through the door and announces: "Good morning, dearie. Now today we are going to sit up in bed and dangle our feet over the side of the bed." You reply: "I take it when you said 'we' you were talking about yourself; surely you did not include me. Can't you see I'm dying? But if you really think I'm going to do any of those things, lady, you have holes in your screen door; your elevator isn't going to the top floor and your motor is about three quarts low on oil."

Guess what happens after all this. You DO sit up in bed and you DO dangle your feet over the side of the bed, and then to cheer you up a little more she announces that tomorrow you will walk—imagine, walk—to the bathroom (you've got to be kidding), and the next day you'll walk to the door, and the day following, "We'll get out in the hall and walk around the corridor, then a little farther every day, and a few days beyond that we'll put you in a wheelchair, take the elevator (a kindly and comforting thought) to the first floor and you'll walk away under your own steam." This is fact, not fiction.

The doctor knows that this kind of therapy works, and the nurse has the doctor on her side. In the "good old days" when a mother went to the hospital to deliver a baby, she stayed for ten days or longer. If you were wealthy enough to buy the hospital, they wouldn't let you stay that long today. Doctors long ago concluded that such lengthy stays in the hospital are a waste of money. They know that the sooner one gets the physical organism out of bed and functioning, no matter how much it hurts, the quicker and more completely it will heal.

Miracles

Tremendous miracles happen in rehab sections of modern hospitals. Muscles and nerves which have been rendered useless because of surgery, disease, accident, or stroke can more often than not be brought back into functioning phase. But therapy always hurts. The therapist gets you down on the floor and tells you to raise your leg as far as you can 25 times, then 30 times, and so on up the scale. Usually you get to the number suggested, and while you are waiting to collapse, she says "Five times more!" The therapist tries to keep us outgrowing ourselves and our abilities.

I remember a TV show a couple of years ago which featured Jim Brady, the man who took the assassin's bullet intended for President Reagan. He's lucky to be alive, but it took hundreds of hours of therapy to get him to where he now is. He had to re-learn how to walk and talk. He referred to it as physical terrorism. I heard him say on that broadcast: "I hope to live long enough to be assured that the most awful room in hell will be reserved for my therapists." Everyone laughed. He probably said it tongue in cheek, because I'm sure he is aware that without all that therapy he wouldn't be anywhere around today.

The doctor does not heal anybody. He only puts things in a certain kind of arrangement or supplies certain bolstering medications so that the body can effectively heal itself. Let's take pneumonia as an example. It used to be a killer disease. Many people never recovered. Today, most of the people who succumb to pneumonia are elderly or those who have AIDS. The modern pneumonia patient is given large doses of penicillin, which spell death for the germ which causes pneumonia. It's like having a whole battalion of new and fresh soldiers added to a tired and almost defeated army within your body. Immediately, these millions of new fighters spread over the body, and in a short time the patient is on the way to recovery. That is the purpose of most medications—to help the body heal itself; the physician is only the facilitator.

Another illustration: How does the doctor treat a broken arm? A broken bone will generally heal without benefit of medical attention, except that after it has healed it might be crooked, or some of the fingers might not work, or the general usefulness of the arm might be impaired. Wherever you go in the civilized world today, a broken arm will be dealt with in almost the same way. The bone will be set, then protected with a cast for six weeks or more. The body must heal itself, but many times the physician-facilitator is needed to help the body perform this function.

Nobody can get you through your grief: no book, no series of lectures, no counselor, no pills, no list of things to do and not do. You have to get yourself through your grief. Of course, all these other things mentioned are facilitators and can help us, and we should avail ourselves of them.

Tears

Tears are necessary. They relieve tensions. One of the laws governing human nature holds that an emotion, once touched off, ushers in a chain of events within the body which must be externalized if the cycle is to be complete. The emotional chain is never complete until the appropriate external reaction occurs. For most of us, the first reaction to the death of a loved one gives rise to a feeling of numbness, shock, disbelief, and tears.

We can conclude from studies made in this field that **there is only one remedy for grief, and that is to grieve.** We should not be ashamed to grieve. We should give vent to grief as we feel it. Jewish people have a custom called shiva, which allows for a week of mourning during which the bereaved and his friends talk about the deceased and his or her virtues. This custom is a wise and healthful one, for there is a close relation between the healing of physical wounds and the healing of emotional wounds. If we are injured, our blood flows freely to cleanse the wound and then heal it. So it is with our grief. If we allow it to flow freely and thereby purge itself, our emotional wound will heal. But if we distort, conceal, or deny our normal feelings, we provide fertile grounds for a breakdown. We should allow a bleeding heart a clean leeway for its expression of grief. Instead of distracting our attention from our bereavement, we should speak of our loss, talk of our sorrow, and eulogize the beauty and virtues of our departed one. There are those who object to a display of grief because they fear that such expression may lead to a nervous collapse. Actually, the opposite is true. Normally, we do not come apart at the seams emotionally as a result of expression or emotional reaction; more often than not, a nervous breakdown results from the repression of emotions. The more we express our grief, the better will be our emotional health in the long run. In essence, we get well by suffering.

People who suppress their grief are deceiving themselves and others into thinking that they are overcoming it. We seldom overcome grief so easily, because it does not dissolve by suppression. It merely slips underground, where it may produce a psychotic illness or cause subtle and damaging changes in our personality.

When we repress any negative emotion (including grief), the emotion is not necessarily dispelled; it may only be building up to volcanic proportions. When the eruption finally does come, the consequences can be more serious than if we had faced and accommodated our original feelings. Feelings walled up within ourselves mean trouble ahead.

Tears are a bereaved person's best friend, an early healing device, a kind of emotional first aid, and sometimes well-meaning friends try to console us with the words "Don't cry." This is the wrong thing to say to a grieving person. Friends are the very ones in whose presence you should be able to cry and feel comfortable doing so. When you don't know what to say to a grieving friend, don't say anything; just listen. It will be like a prayer of benediction, and will show how understanding you really are.

What we are talking about is the second task which we must perform in order to recover from our grief—the need to experience the pain of grief.

"But," someone might say, "if the responses during impact are automatic, how could an individual not make the choice to experience grief fully?"

That's the paradox. The automatic, natural responses occur, but we decide whether to experience these responses or to stifle and suppress them.

And there are many reasons why we might choose to suppress our grief instead of expressing it. The pain might seem unbearable. It may seem more reasonable, since nothing can be done about the loss, to try to forget it, to put it behind us as quickly as possible. People around us may encourage us to "be brave," "be strong," to "pull yourself together." Crying is not the opposite of being strong. We may feel that if we don't rise above the loss, we are denying tenets of faith or a philosophy we have affirmed and lived by. Perhaps people around us indicate—and we ourselves may believe—that sufficient time has passed for us to be finished with our grieving. We may be embarrassed to express our grief in front of others. We may curtail it, because it is interfering with our daily activities.

All these reasons not to choose to experience and express our grief fully can be found in our own reluctance to feel the pain of grief and in the general attitude toward grieving that is present in our culture. Author Elizabeth Harper Neeld, in her book *Seven Choices,* makes the statement: "And society gives us little permission to grieve. We know that the better we appear to be coping, the easier it is for people to be around us. We know what people want to hear are reports such as 'holding up well,' 'She went back to work on Monday.' The anthropologist Geoffrey Gorer says it bluntly: 'Mourning is treated as if it were a weakness, a self-indulgence, a reprehensible habit instead of a psychological necessity.'"

Tears are important in the nurturing of the spirit, but do we really understand the function and meaning of them? God gave us tears for a purpose. If the eyes have no tears, the soul has no rainbow. There are few things as comforting and soothing as the consoling effect of quiet tears, for tears have the power to dissolve the many tensions inherent in our experiences with sorrow. Tears, warm and wet, are soothing and can do much to help cleanse the painful wounds of our lives.

We should not be ashamed of legitimate tears or feel guilty about shedding them. We may discover that we can see farther through a tear than through a telescope. Our tears may be crystallized into lenses through which we can better see God's purpose for us and our loved ones. Weeping can be appropriate, noble, and majestic.

Dr. Joyce Brothers, the well-known psychologist, counselor, and writer, in her book *Widowed,* reports some scientific experiments which have been done in recent years revealing that tears of anger and sadness contain leucine-enkephalin, one of the brain's natural pain relievers. They also found that tears contain prolactin, a hormone which encourages the secretion of tears. They learned that women have half again as much prolactin as men, which might explain in part why women cry more than men do.

"Before these latest experiments, scientists had discovered the presence of prolactin and leucine-enkephalin in the central nervous system. According to Dr. William Frey II, biochemist and research director of the Dry Eye and Tear Research Center at the St. Paul-Ramsey Center in Minneapolis, the scientists could find no reason why these brain chemicals were found in tears.

Dr. Frey believes that crying triggers the brain to release these chemicals "because it is an exocrine process in which a substance like sweat or urine or feces comes out of the body, cleansing it of toxic substances. There is reason to believe that crying does the same thing." Dr. Frey says "crying does not just feel good, it appears to be an evolutionary device for adapting to emotional stress. When a person is sad or angry, crying automatically removes the chemicals that build up during stress and helps one feel better." Many years ago, Dr. Karl Menninger wrote: "Weeping is perhaps the most human and universal of all relief measures."

It is not unreasonable to assume that people have cried ever since the human race came on the scene. In the Talmud we find the story which illustrates the importance of tears: "When God banished Adam and Eve from the Garden of Eden, Adam protested that the punishment was too severe. They would not be able to cope with the world outside the Garden of Eden.

"God considered Adam's plea and found it valid, so he gave Adam and Eve two gifts to help them cope with the hardships of the world. The first gift was the Sabbath for rest and contemplation, the second was the tear."

The tears of a survivor are varied; they may spring from sadness, frustration, self-pity, even of anger. All are parts of the grief process. On the other hand, the shedding of tears can become a habit, and a bad one at that. If you discover that you cry at certain times of the day or under certain circumstances, you need to do something—anything that will defuse the situation—call someone on the telephone, make the bed, walk around the block, read a good book—anything to keep your emotional train of thought on the right track.

Pavlov, the Russian physiologist, became famous for his experiments with dogs and their responses to various stimuli. At feeding time, he would first ring a bell and then set out the food. After a while, he noted that the dogs began to salivate whenever they heard the bell. After they had become accustomed to the routine—the bell, then the food—he rang the bell but gave them no food. They still salivated whenever they heard the bell.

Of course we are not dogs, but our reaction patterns are formed in much the same way. When a certain set of circumstances (the mention of the decedent's name) occurs, we cry. You can learn how to change this by "not answering the bell." You have to make up your mind to do it, and it takes practice and vigilance, but it works.

It is quite possible that the above explanation provides more than you really wanted to know about tears, but it does have a point, and perhaps knowing these facts will help you to not feel so ashamed of your tears.

Talk

Talking about our sorrow helps release tension and dissolve the pain of the grief experience. It is true that each time we talk about a painful experience, our pain is eased just a little more. As we talk, we heal. It is by speaking to others of our loss and sorrow that we learn to bear pain. In time, memories of our loved one will come back to us, but their power to hurt will have dissipated.

Talking has a therapeutic value. First, it is cathartic. When we verbalize, we help release the pent-up tensions resulting from grief. An angry man yells; a terrified woman screams; and a bereaved person sheds tears and talks. Through verbalization, our feelings of loss, loneliness, guilt, anger, and hostility toward the departed are brought to the surface of our consciousness where we can deal with them. In one of our groups, a recently widowed lady in her early thirties said that her greatest problem was that "no one would let me talk about my loss. They all feel that my talking about it would bring the reality of the loss back to me. They just don't realize that I have to talk in order to get through it."

In the second place, talking provides us with insight, which enables us to see more clearly our real feelings and problems. We should not be afraid of verbalizing our feelings of anger and hostility toward our loved ones, because they too possessed the weaknesses and failings of mankind. No one is perfect. Only after we have achieved this insight will we discover that new feelings and reactions will be forthcoming.

In the third place, the talking process establishes a wholesome relationship with the persons in whom we confide. In a very real sense, they help us bear our sorrow by knowing our feelings about it.

A few words of caution should be spoken at this point concerning the expression of our grief. First of all, when the death of a loved one interrupts our normal pattern of life, we may try to cope with our loss by rationalizing. We may attempt to exercise extreme self-control, acting as though nothing had happened. We may seek new interests in life and exhibit great bursts of energy and enthusiasm as we become overly busy in our efforts to avoid loneliness and memories. Some of us may seek to "cover up" by embarking on some kind of a binge, forgetting that we cannot drink, smoke, work, play, or eat our way out of grief, nor find the solution to any of our problems by carrying on any activity solely for escape.

A second word of caution has to do with a tendency and temptation to syndicate our sorrows. They should not be shared with everyone we meet. We recall the story of a boy who had an injured thumb and told everyone he met about his hurt as he painfully unwound the bandage before the eyes of all who would listen to his tale of woe. His sore thumb dominated not only his horizon but also the horizons of all who knew him. Every time they thought of him, they remembered his sore thumb. So with us; how much better it would be for us and our friends if, when they think of us, they would think of us not as being obsessed by sorrow, but as courageously mastering it.

In the third place, we must be careful that the social pressures of our culture do not prohibit us from doing the kind of mourning that will have a therapeutic effect. Our culture has a rather highly developed pattern which our reactions to grief should follow. There are certain established duties required of us who are mourners. We often curtail and restrict our social activities and dress somberly in a mode symbolic of the feelings a bereaved person should have. We mourners may thereby find ourselves between the two horns of a dilemma. On the one hand, we may feel the necessity for the "proper amount of tears" to demonstrate and prove our affection for the departed; and on the other hand, we may try to "bear up wonderfully." Despite the fact that during the past few generations our culture has made much progress in a better direction, it is still necessary to satisfy the social demands for a particular type of mourning which may be superficial and have little regard for our true feelings. We may also be substituting this type of surface mourning for the deeper experience of grieving which is really necessary, and we may thereby fail to find real and permanent healing. The proper response to our loss will probably be the one that comes most naturally.

The final word of warning has to do with an excessive display of grief. There is a thought-provoking passage in Jewish rabbinical wisdom that says: "It is impossible not to mourn, but to mourn excessively is forbidden." Excessive grief is seldom a genuine way of showing devotion to our departed loved one. Would it please your loved one to see you so completely given over to sorrow that you are beside yourself to the point where no one can do anything with you or for you? Excessive grief more often than not brings in its wake deterioration of the personality, upset digestion, malfunctioning of the bodily organs, and a general impairment of health.

In the Jewish Talmud there is a story of a man who had a little girl, his only child, who became sick and died. His heart was broken. Despite all the efforts of his friends to comfort him and help him realize that life does go on, he refused to be comforted.

One night he dreamed that he was in heaven and saw little girls in a pageant. Each girl carried a lighted candle. The candle carried by his own daughter was unlit. As he took her in his arms and caressed her he asked, "Why is your candle not lit?" She answered, "Sometimes it does light, but your tears always put it out."

It is natural for us to be disturbed, heartbroken and concerned when a loved one is taken from us. But to despair overmuch and to be unwilling to recognize God and the eternal life he gives us is both unwise and unhealthy. The sun always rises to shine through the clouds after the darkest night, but constant tears and lamenting will prevent us from ever seeing the light.

"Rose Kennedy, who faced many tragedies in her 104 years, said: 'I have always believed that God never gives a cross to bear larger than we can carry. No matter what, He wants us to be happy, not sad. Birds sing after a storm. Why shouldn't we?'" (Cleveland Amory in *Parade*).

1. The Rituals of Mourning

I do not want to be overly critical about the lack of funerary rites which are being promoted in our day—no embalming, no visitation at the mortuary, no funeral, memorial services, etc. They call it quick disposal. While to some people this may seem to be the quickest, easiest, and least expensive way to dispose of the body of a loved one, there is good reason to believe that it's not the best way to proceed because it denies the survivors the needed opportunity and right to mourn and to grant their loved one the "rite of passage." Following the quick disposal method denies family and friends the opportunity for a last goodbye.

Our Jewish friends keep the seven days of shiva, staying in their homes, while bereaved Chinese families are homebound for a month after a loved one has passed away and their friends come and visit them. The procedures most of us follow or choose in giving our loved ones the rite of passage have value! For most mourners, the visitation at the mortuary, which usually occurs during the day or evening prior to the funeral, is a difficult and threatening situation, but during that visitation friends and loved ones offer comfort by embracing you and crying with you. When it is all over, you feel satisfied that you did the right thing. You had a chance to ventilate your feelings with people who love and understand. "Having a body, a casket, or a grave helps us focus our grief and recognize the finality of our loss."

What do you do with a Bible that is so torn and worn that it is no longer useful? The custom of our day says it should be burned in a clean fire. What do we do with a public building that is going to be torn down? Before the bulldozer arrives on the scene, the cornerstone is opened and the contents are ceremonially removed. What do we do with a Navy ship that is old and worn out and no longer capable of being a fighting ship? We hold a decommissioning service—the flag is lowered, the ship's log and bell are removed, along with some other things before the vessel is reduced to scrap metal.

2. The Body

The Bible teaches that the body is the temple of God, a place where God dwells: "You are the temple of God." "Your body is the temple of the Holy Spirit" (I Corinthians 3:16 and 6:19). When it is worn out and the spirit no longer dwells within it, do you just dispose of it in the quickest and easiest way? Is it wrong to believe that the loved one is entitled to some rites of passage? There should be some kind of observance or ceremony indicating that someone is no longer present and we will miss them. And to prove that we really mean it, we might choose to further memorialize the person by setting up a memorial fund, or trust or foundation, that will continue to bless mankind. Incidentally, humans are the only creatures who erect memorials to their dead.

3. Thank-You Notes, Etc.

Another step in the acceptance of your loss is the writing of personal notes of thanks to those who brought food, sent flowers, contributed to a memorial fund or helped you in any way. This is a difficult thing to do, but it should not be unduly postponed. People will not judge you for taking a little extra time, because they realize that there are other and more pressing duties which you must attend to. While we're talking about taking your time, take a little more time and write a personal note as well as your name. Just say, "Thank you for taking your time to be with me in my most difficult hour." It will bring tears as you write to certain cherished friends, but that's okay.

In addition to the thank-you notes, there will be the memorial book to be filled out, newspaper clippings you may want to keep and special letters that brought comfort to you. All these activities will help you in accepting your loss.

4. Review the Life

Many people find it very rewarding to write an evaluation of the life and contributions of their loved one. This should not be done in haste; take plenty of time, because it will be a word portrait of your loved one and you will want it to be a best effort. You might gather some of your material from the eulogy that was given at the service, tributes which others shared with you, and interesting bits of conversation relating to your loved one. A widower in one of our grief groups related that after he had written a poem about his wife, his soul felt purged—cleansed. Try to recall the total life—the painful as well as the joyful. Every picture is made up of dark as well as light colors. All of us have some ambivalence toward our loved ones and friends; nobody is perfect. Shakespeare had Marc Antony say in *Julius Caesar:* "The evil that men do lives after them; the good is often interred with their bones." It is equally true to say that "the good that men do lives after them; the bad is often interred with their bones." We decide whether the good or the bad will predominate in our memories of anyone.

I remember Nola, an 80-years-plus lady, who had been widowed about five years when I first met her. As an interim pastor, I had called at her home several times. Never did I hear her complain that the Lord took her Jack after more than 50 years of marriage. I never heard her whimper or cry. What I really remember about her was that she was constantly telling me all the wonderful things that she and Jack had done together through the years, places they had visited and vacations they had. She was following Dale Carnegie's advice: "Count your blessings—not your burdens." We all can profit from following such advice. It was this characteristic which made Nola such a special and upbeat person. A visit to her home always gave me a lift.

Looking at albums of photographs will help you remember. Just a word of caution: Excessive review of the loved one's life might indicate a need for professional help. Looking at the past may be comforting and helpful, but we must not forget that we also have a future. The future is neither bright nor inviting for one who lives in a cemetery or with a dead loved one constantly in one's thoughts. It was Charles F. Kettering who said: "You can't have a better tomorrow if you are thinking about yesterday all the time."

5. Keep a Journal

A device that will help you discern whether you are making progress is to keep a journal or diary of your feelings, and you should begin keeping this journal as soon as possible. This is one of the best investments you make in your journey. Write down your feelings—all of them, the good and the bad. There is something that happens when you put your thoughts down on paper. Somewhere down the path you may suddenly be plunged into a relapse which makes it seem as though your loss had occurred only yesterday, and you go around in a circle of self-pity and crying which may last for a matter of minutes, an hour, a whole day, or it could spoil a whole week. Little wonder that you should feel you haven't made any progress. It seems you've moved forward three paces and then slipped back two, and you say to yourself, "I'll never get through this." Before you do anything rash, read the first entries in your journal. Most people can hardly believe that they actually wrote these words. "Did I really feel that badly? I can't remember that it was that awful and that I was so hopeless." But there is the record. You wrote it down yourself, and the fact that those awful experiences and emotions are recorded there will indicate to you that you have made progress. Remember—it wasn't someone else who wrote those entries. Relapses are normal experiences. You are not responsible for bringing them on, because they are usually caused by people or agents outside of yourself.

Bob Deits in *Life After Loss* suggests that in addition to things which you might think to put in your journal, you might also want to include some of the following:

1. A significant event that occurred today.
2. The person who was the most important to me today.
3. Changes I observe happening to me.
4. My plans for tomorrow include...
5. Notes to myself.

6. Bibliotherapy—Therapy from Reading

The more we understand and become acquainted with the processes of grief, the better we will be able to cope with it. Books have been tools for preventing and solving problems as long as books and problems have been in existence. There is a book for most anything you want to know about. We attend classes and read books to learn how to cook, sew, change a spark plug, and many other things. In recent years there has been a flood of books on grief and how to deal with it. But books need to be read and studied. In reading you will discover what is normal and learn how others have handled the problems of bereavement, and you will come to identify with others who walk the same road. The author becomes your counselor. On the lintel of the doorway of the library of Thebes, the capital of Egypt prior to 1375 B.C., are inscribed these words: "The healing place of the soul." In diligent reading you will find many others who coped with the problem of grief; discover that your emotions are normal, and you will be encouraged.

Needless to say, while you are in the acute suffering phase of grieving, your comprehension span and ability to concentrate are greatly impaired. Maybe you won't quite understand what the author is saying until you have read the paragraph many times. Keep at it; your power to comprehend and concentrate will improve. And when you come across an idea that sounds productive and logical and one which you could employ, use it. Try it; if it worked for someone else, it might also work for you. Knowledge alone is not wisdom. When we make the knowledge personal by applying what we learn from what we read by applying it to ourselves—that is wisdom.

Joanne Bernstein in *Loss and How to Cope with It* says, "No matter who is doing the reading, devouring scores of books will never amount to a pill you can take to replace the labor needed for answering the cruel questions of bereavement. They can be part of your effort." Grief will not go away by itself any more than our earthquake-shaken house can put itself back together again. You have to work at it.

7. Parting with Clothes and Possessions

Sorting through all the "things" your loved one left behind is a necessary part of letting go. How long should you wait to do this? There are no set rules, but most counselors would agree that it should be taken care of as soon as possible, and it should be done by you, not delegated to others. I know of one widow whose husband's clothes were still in the closet thirteen years after he had died. When you feel that you are ready, why not invite a close friend or relative, or another member of the family, to be with you, one in whose presence you could cry without being embarrassed. You might also decide to do it alone. One widow I know did it this way: After coming home from church one Sunday, about two months after her loss, she gathered a lot of boxes and cartons, sorted everything out and stacked them on the living room floor. About five o'clock that same day her daughter, who lives nearby, walked in the door and said to her mother: "What have you done? Why didn't you call me to come and help you?" Her mother replied: "I looked in the clothes closets and decided that there were just too many clothes, so I went to work and did it." To each her own.

In *Endings and Beginnings,* Sandra Aldrich advises: "Part of the work of grief is coming to terms with the 'things' which the deceased has left behind—clothes, toys, papers and other possessions. To live among these belongings as if the person were still around to use them is as much a distortion of reality as the attempt to wipe out all the evidence of that life." You must decide for yourself what memories you can handle, and put out of sight the things you cannot live with.

John W. James and Frank Cherry in *The Grief Recovery Handbook* make the following suggestions: "First of all, put everything which belonged to the deceased in one room; then designate at least three piles:

1. The things you are certain you want to keep because they have special significance or utilitarian value. They go back in the closet. Special mementos should be hidden away in drawers or other available hiding places. Make a list of where you placed every item. Pictures which might bring tears should be in a place where they are not in your view most of the time.

2. The things you are certain you want to dispose of by giving them to relatives and friends who would appreciate them. If seeing another person wearing them would unduly upset you, give them to the Salvation Army, Goodwill, medical centers, thrift stores, or other organizations which deal in such things. Why hoard what others might need and could put to good use?

3. The things you are not certain about. Store these in the attic, basement, or garage where they will be out of sight most of the time. Ideas will come to you from time to time about what you should do with some of them.

Take your time. Don't be too hasty about those decisions. Later you might have second thoughts about some of them, but if they are in other hands, it will be too late. Sandra Aldrich also said: "To part with those things (associated with precious memories) before the griever is ready can complicate the letting-go process."

Following a plan like this, you will have made a selective and sensible disposition of the possessions of your loved one.

In one of my Grief Recovery Seminars, a senior lady stood before the group as she said: "This Pendleton jacket was my husband's favorite. It fits me fine, so I decided to wear it myself. Every time I put it on I feel his hands putting it in place over my shoulder. The belt which holds my slacks up was his, and it fits me. Whenever I put it on, I feel his arms around my waist." Granted, not every widow can do this, but wouldn't it be wonderful if you could add this dimension to your life? Try it!

After you have finished this difficult and tearful task, treat yourself to something nice: Take your closest friend to dinner and celebrate, or take a holiday at some nice place away from home. In all probability you will enjoy it more if you don't go alone.

8. Postpone Major Decisions

It's a good idea to wait at least a year or perhaps even two years before you consider selling the house. If the house is too big for you to care for, or the mortgage payments are too burdensome, it might be wise to move to smaller quarters. It's always a good idea to seek counsel from people who have expertise in these matters and others whose opinions you value. It's bad enough to lose your mate, but losing your home is an added burden of sorrow. The same may be true of keeping your job if you have one. Matters relating to property should be discussed with your financial advisor or banker or a good friend who has experience in such things.

Another decision you may have to make is about your engagement and wedding rings. When do you move them to the other hand? No one can answer this question for you, and no one can tell you that you have to do it. Genevieve Ginsburg in *To Live Again* says, "After six months I looked at the ring; I realized that I was no longer married. I had no husband. It had to come off, so I would say goodbye not only to him, but to that which was."

Your engagement and wedding rings are links to your own memories and are to be worn or removed as you please. If you make a decision about removing them, then you might first of all try wearing them on the other hand for an hour or so or longer. If that doesn't give you too much of a guilt problem, lengthen the time and you will come to accept it. It should be said that if you have any plans to remarry—and right now you probably don't—the sooner the rings go off the better; their presence on your left hand might indicate that you are not available.

Many women have solved this problem by having the engagement and wedding rings melted down and refashioned into something else, which you might choose to wear yourself, or it might be treasured by a daughter or granddaughter. If you wear it yourself, the continuity with the past and the sentiment it engenders are preserved. Only the form is changed. If the husband is the survivor, he must make these decisions about the rings and other jewelry his wife wore.

One author quotes a widow in this regard: "I was married for 46 years and I don't intend to get married again. This ring is part of my hand; my husband put it there, and there it's going to stay."

Avoid making far-reaching decisions hastily, like moving in with other members of your family. Be independent as long as you can. If you can look after yourself and your family agrees, it's the right thing to do, because when you move in with one of your children, in-laws or friends, you are no longer the queen or king of your castle. It's someone else's home, and things will go the way *they* want them to go, and not necessarily the way you would want them to go. You might be thinking that you just can't and don't want to live alone. Consider your options. If you are a senior citizen, it might be well to look at some of the affordable retirement homes which have been built in so many communities in recent years.

9. Thank God for Your Work and Other Things That Keep You Busy

Thank God for having things to do which occupy your mind and keep you busy. Of course, in the early days of your bereavement there will be a host of things, legal and otherwise, which will occupy much of your time. After these have been taken care of, try to get your life back on track.

I have heard many widows say, "My job was my salvation. I had to get up every day and go to work, or I had to get the kids to school every day, pack their lunches, do the laundry, keep up the house, do the grocery shopping, etc." Drudgery can sometimes be a blessing. Keeping busy is therapeutic. But avoid the kind of busyness or frantic activity that produces nothing. Later on we will discuss the possibility of your becoming a volunteer if you have some hours or days of a week to invest in making our world a better place. I'm not thinking of stuffing envelopes, licking stamps, etc., but rather the kind of activity in which you are actually dealing with people and personally helping someone else.

Basically, we have two options: Forget everything and run, or face everything and recover. Some people just start out running. Many who are widowed or divorced go on trips and cruises, one after another. All this, in an effort to forget, really amounts to running away. You can't run forever, because when you get back the same problem will still confront you. It's better to face it head-on on your home turf. Trips are expensive. You need to work on the problem from the inside. Running away once in awhile, to be alone, see new things or just to get your head together, is okay up to a point, but don't make a habit of it. Do the things you need to do.

10. Resolving Anger and Guilt

Anger is a part of the experience of many people who lose a loved one, but it should also be said that not everyone who loses a loved one is angry. Don't be upset if you are angry, and don't be worried and think you're peculiar if you're not.

If anger is present, the first thing we need to do in dealing with it is to find out who it is we are angry with: the doctor, the nurses, the funeral director, the clergyman, God, ourselves, and even the loved one who has died and left us to deal with all these problems. The person who is now gone would not have caused the death, unless it was a suicide, but maybe we and they knew they should give up cigarettes or alcohol or drugs, and live more healthy lives, but they refused. That is a good reason for us to be angry.

The next thing we need to do to defuse the anger is to go to the person and have a face-to-face meeting. If it's the loved one you recently buried, go to the cemetery or mausoleum and pour out your anger. You may not get any answers, but you will feel better.

Mary Jane's husband had passed away about six months prior to her telling our grief group, amidst many tears, how angry she was at the doctor and everyone else who had anything to do with her husband's care, but especially the doctor.

I suggested that she needed to talk with him. She countered with statements like "He won't take time to talk with me or listen to my story. I'm not anyone in his sight, and besides, he's chief of staff this year." I held my ground—she needed to talk with that doctor. Several weeks later she informed the group that she had made an appointment with the doctor.

At our next meeting, she gave an ecstatic report of her visit. "He listened to me; he never argued; he answered questions about the treatment procedures, and when I walked out of that hospital I said to myself, 'He's the kindest man I ever met.'" Admittedly, it doesn't always work out that well, but it is a positive step.

If the person lives far away, write a letter. Over a period of several days, put down the things you want to say, then write it; keep it on top of the desk for a few days to do some editing so you will not need to be ashamed of what you said. Then send it.

Sometimes we have reason to be angry with God. Norma's father died in his early fifties of natural causes. She was a sincere and consistent Christian and couldn't understand why she had been wrestling with this loss for so many months. One day she confided to her husband that she was really angry with God about her loss; he inquired whether she had ever told God about her feelings. She replied that she didn't think it would be proper. Then he asked her, "Do you think God would come unglued if you told Him how you feel?"

Several days later she went to the cemetery, stood by her father's grave, looked up to heaven, and prayed, "God, I'm angry with you for letting this happen to me." She reports that it helped her. This approach is not new. I believe that listening to our anger is one of God's ways of helping us with our healing. After all, isn't He the Wonderful Counselor? Tell Him how badly you feel and ask for His grace in helping you understand and accept it. Allow yourself to feel these emotions. It's always okay to ask God "WHY."

Most everyone who loses a loved one may have guilt feelings relating to that loss. These are the "if onlys." If only we had called a doctor sooner, or had the surgery he had suggested, or even changed doctors. If only I had not left him alone that last night, etc. All things considered, I believe that most of us did the very best we knew at the time; we used our best judgment. Maybe we had too little time to gather second opinions. Hindsight is always 20-20 vision; it's the foresight we have the problems with, because it's so clouded. If we did the best we knew under the circumstances, who could do any better or more than that? We should not have to assume the responsibility for our loved one's death. The "if onlys" are the hallmark of grief, and too often we braid them into a whip of remorse, and remorse is a dead end on the grieving road. <u>Note it well!</u>

One of the things we need to do toward resolving guilt is to ascertain whether the guilt is real or false. If the guilt is real, we need to face it and make amends if possible. We might find solace in confession and learn that forgiveness awaits us. But what if the person we are guilty of hurting is no longer around to hear our confession and grant us forgiveness?

Many people have found comfort in writing a letter to the person they have hurt. In your letter you made the confession. That was the most you could do. You cleansed your own soul in that confession; now you need to forgive yourself and go on with your life.

One day I had just concluded a graveside service for an elderly mother of four grown daughters and a son. Before departing, the son came to me with this confession: "Mother made it very clear to all of us that she wanted no funeral service. She wished to be cremated and have her remains scattered over the ocean. No one in our family had ever been cremated, to our knowledge. We just could not go along with her wishes; we did just what she did not want us to do, and we're feeling very guilty about it. What can we do to work our way through this?"

At first glance, we would say that they were guilty of disobeying their mother. They had done the opposite of what she had asked of them. I tried to explain to the son that funeral services are held for the benefit of the living, not for the dead. I asked but did not answer the question: "Does the decedent have the right to tell her loved ones how they should mourn?" Whatever funerary practices we follow are intended to give our loved one "the rite of passage." It provides closure. It's saying, "It's all right to go."

When he pressed me for something his family might do to atone for their disobedience to their mother, I suggested that all five of them come to the grave some day. Either choose one person as the spokesperson or let each one speak audibly something like: "Mother, we appreciate everything you have done for us. You have been a good mother. All of us feel conscience-stricken in having disobeyed your last wishes; cremation sounded so repulsive to us; we just couldn't go through with it, and we want to feel that you forgive us." If the guilt is real, it needs to be resolved, because unresolved guilt can last a lifetime, and that adds up to a lot of misery.

Imogene had expressed to our group many times her total lack of self-esteem, which she interpreted as being due to the guilt she had carried around all of her life. She was the last of five girls born to her parents. "My father never let me forget that I was supposed to have been a boy. I have dragged this around all those years." As the leader of the group, I inquired of her: "Did anyone ever tell you that the sex of a child is determined by the father? It is a scientific fact." Her bittersweet response was: "And how many years I've wasted worrying about that!"

Imogene's experience is a true example of false guilt. Things are not always what we think they are. Something you saw in the backyard on a moonlight night looked like a ghost to you, but upon closer examination it was just a pair of long johns which someone had hung on the line to dry. It might be a good idea to check out our feelings in an effort to discover whether they are based on fact or fiction. Feelings of anger and guilt will not go away by themselves; we have to work at them.

11. Join a Support Group

No one can help you as much as someone who has been or is now traveling the same road you are now on. You need new friends who are going through the same experience. Join a support group made up of people who are engaged in the same struggle you are. They really know how you feel. Find the support groups in your area and decide which one seems right for you, and attend a time or two to get the feel of the group before you join. Don't wait. The worst thing you can do right now is to do nothing. Grief will not go away by itself, even with the passing of time. Take a step; something good may happen. If you don't take a step, nothing will happen. Once you become a part of such a group, you will be gratified by the feelings of caring and support that will be yours. Make an effort to form intimate friendships within the group; take advantage of the opportunity to do things together with them. Having such a focus outside yourself will help you to do more than merely survive.

12. Return to Normal Activities as Soon as Possible

The first time you return to activities you normally shared with your loved one will be the most difficult. If you return to normal functions quite soon after your loss, some people might be embarrassed by your presence and might not know what to say to you. Don't let it bother you; they will get accustomed to it and will give you credit for being very brave. Try to talk and act naturally, avoiding the subject of your loss. Each time it will be a little easier, and you will begin to feel better about how you are handling it.

Dottie and her husband had spent a part of every day walking together through the mall near their home. She had come into one of our groups several months before sharing with us the difficulties she had in going back and walking through the mall. She felt it would be too difficult ever to do it again. After several months in our group, she made the decision to try it.

Had she asked me about it, I might have suggested that she go in the company of a dear friend in whose presence she would not be embarrassed or ashamed to break down in tears. But she did not ask me;

she decided on her own. She shared with our group: "I watered down the sidewalks of every shop in the place with my tears, but I kept on going. When I got back to the parking lot, my eyes were so bleary with so much crying that I had difficulty in finding my car. I repeated the therapy the next day, and the day after that, and have continued it every day. Now, when I walk the mall, I don't cry any more. I do regret his not being with me, but as I walk I feel his presence by my side." That's what happens when you decide to become a victor rather than a victim.

Mary, one of our neighbors, nursed her husband through a long and difficult illness. During this time, she was homebound and disassociated from her friends. About two years after his passing, she remarked to me: "I'm back doing the things I used to do with Bob and associating with people of my past life." That's progress! She was better and not bitter, and you can be, too.

Sometimes in getting back with former associates you might have to stiffen your emotional backbone a bit and put on a little bravado. That's okay so long as you know you are not denying your loss. It's somewhat like watching a duck make its way upstream through turbulent waters. Everything you can see looks normal and unruffled, but underneath you know that little duck is paddling like the dickens.

Each time you succeed in getting back with old friends, your own self-esteem will be enhanced and you will feel better about how you are handling your loss.

13. Take Care of Yourself

Going through an experience of sorrow can be a threat to your health. Some people don't eat right or regularly, mostly because they just don't feel like it. Everything seems tasteless. Right now you may not feel like taking care of yourself, but that will eventually change if you really decide that it should and you work at it. You are the most important person in the world to yourself; your life is valuable; take care of it.

There will be times when you will have to force yourself to cook and then sit down to a full meal. Following some types of abdominal surgical procedures, a patient may have difficulty in getting the appetite back on track. Nothing tastes good and you have no appetite. Lucille had this problem. Following gallbladder surgery she was served three meals every day, none of which she ever touched. She was slowly starving herself to death. Then one day, at the time of the evening meal, her doctor followed the nurse into her room. The nurse placed the dinner stand beside Lucille's bed and left. The doctor pulled a chair near to the bed and announced: "I'm sitting here until all the food on that tray is inside you. So get with it." And she did. Her battle was won, and she progressed rapidly after that.

There is some truth in the statement that the worst-fed women in the world are widows. Some studies indicate that one-third of them are eating below the poverty level. Your body needs nourishment now, more than ever. If eating alone is a chore, why not have some good friends come in and share a meal with you? Several women in the same situation could get together and, with a little planning, they could eat one meal in a different home every day. Remember—there are others out there who are struggling with the same thing you are.

Watching the TV or listening to the radio or reading the newspaper helps some people get through mealtimes. Get dressed every day. I've heard more than one widow say that she never put on a dress for more than a month after her husband died. Something like this really sends your self-image down the tube. You are the only person who can build your self-image. You need to feel good about yourself and what you are doing, and sometimes it's very much of an uphill battle.

Do something nice for yourself. Buy some new clothes. Have your hair done professionally and regularly. Get a manicure or pedicure or massage. Baby yourself a bit; no one else is going to do it. Dress up and go out, even if it's just to show yourself that you can do it.

Exercise regularly. You don't need hundreds of dollars' worth of equipment to do it. Walking is the best, least expensive, and most beneficial exercise we know of. (But because we live in dangerous times, it is not wise to walk alone, even in the daytime, unless there are plenty of people nearby.)

14. Exercise Your Faith and Hope

Someone has said that a person who doesn't have faith is as handicapped as a person who has no feet. Sorrow looks back, worry looks ahead; faith looks up.

A short time ago, Terry Anderson, one of the former hostages in Lebanon, said on a TV program in response to someone's question about what he would like to do to his captors who had stolen five or six years from his life: "I am a Christian and a Catholic. I am more interested in forgiving my enemies than I am in wanting to punish them." He certainly had many reasons for wanting retribution. That is faith in action. Take advantage of your religious faith if you have one. If you have become inactive, become involved again. The Bible has a great deal to say about sorrow—not how to circumvent it, but how to get through it. We don't always practice the things we say we believe. It's a lot better to hope than not to hope. Hope and faith are attitudes which we can develop, but we have to build these attitudes and then act upon them.

The following incident occurred on an Easter Sunday some years ago as a father and his son were walking home from church. The son of the Sunday school superintendent had died that week. Probably no one had expected him to be in church that day. But there he was; he directed the opening service, taught his class and then sang in the choir at the worship service. The little boy asked his father: "How could he have done that when he buried his son a few days before?" The father replied, "Well, isn't that what Easter is all about—resurrection and life after death? All Christians believe that we will see each other again, don't they?" After a few thoughtful moments, the boy responded, "But not like that, Dad. Not like that."

People who exercise this kind of faith have a great deal of inner bracing that keeps them from crumbling in the hour of stress—just like the steel ribs of a giant submarine. It is built so strong that it can descend into great depths of the ocean without being crushed by the tremendous pressure exerted upon it.

Early in my ministry I served as a pastor of a church in West Hollywood, California. Down the street a couple of blocks from our church there was a decorator's shop. Howard Verbeck, the owner, had helped our church many times. When we needed a new dossal curtain, he designed and made it for us. When we were planning the redecoration of our sanctuary he advised us on colors, etc. Through the years we became good friends. Then one year he lost both his wife and his only child, a twenty-two-year-old daughter who had never married nor made him a grandfather. Those were two very great losses in so short a time. I never heard him complain about his lot. His life seemed to go on. I never heard him ask, "Why me?" Then one day I felt compelled to ask him how he had so well dealt with his great losses. He replied: "Well, Stan, I can't say exactly how it happened, but through it all **the Lord gave me a great healing.**" When the Lord heals you, you will know that you are healed and you can be assured that our life can go on. Howard and I did not have the same religious profession or background, but I couldn't argue about how he had come through this time so well.

In a recent issue of the daily devotional *Our Daily Bread,* Herbert Vander Lugt offers this insight: "The writer of Psalm 42 had many reasons to be discouraged. He was living in exile many miles north of

Jerusalem. He was taunted by people who didn't believe in God. The sound of rushing water among the boulders and over falls on the slopes of Mount Hermon symbolized for his vivid imagination the wave after wave of sorrow that engulfed him. How he longed to join the worshippers in the temple. Yet, he told himself to trust in God (verse 5), and he ended the psalm on a note of victory. As he laid aside his writing tool, his circumstances were no different. But he was!"

"The same thing can happen to us. No matter what our circumstance, little by little, faith can win over depression. The important change is the change God works in our heart."

15. Become a Volunteer

In a recent television interview, Dr. Joyce Brothers quoted the testimony of Dr. James House of the University of Michigan: "If you volunteer and work to help others, you actually live longer. A ten-year survey indicates that those people who do not volunteer, who do not help others, are two and a half times more likely to die within a period of time than those who have physically helped others."

When you start giving yourself to someone else's need, you will feel differently about yourself. Helping carry someone else's load is guaranteed to lighten your own. You can turn your loss into gain by transforming your suffering into service. When you feel yourself getting depressed, call on someone who is alone and lonely or suffering the battles of life. In this way you can translate your despair into compassionate hope and love. You will probably never know what you gave them, but you will know that in the doing something happened within you. It always happens that way. It is impossible to give of yourself without receiving something in return.

Author Philomene Gates in *Suddenly Alone* counsels: "[Helping] others is the primary reason for living. Ninety million Americans have already discovered the fulfillment that volunteerism can bring. It enhances the self-esteem, fosters a sense of accomplishment and worthiness and is an antidote for depression. Volunteers live healthier, happier, and longer than non-volunteers. Service to others is what life's all about. You don't have to turn into a Joan of Arc or don a hair shirt and give up all your luxuries. If you contribute something to society on a regular basis, you will be a richer person."

There are dozens of organizations in your area which depend on the work of volunteers to better serve the community. Everyone can help someone. Social-service involvement is good for your health.

To sum it up: The work of grieving has two phases—acceptance of the loss and healing the wound which caused the loss. It was Albert Pike who said, **"What we do for ourselves dies with us. What we do for others remains and is immortal."**

When I was four years old I broke my left elbow. For six weeks my left arm was immobilized in a plaster cast. On the evening of the day the doctor removed it, my father asked me to lay my left arm on the dinner table. He placed his strong blacksmith's hand on my biceps and explained that the doctor had ordered that my left elbow was to be bent so that the forearm was almost parallel with the biceps. He assured me that this would hurt, which I already knew, because I had done a little experimenting on my own.

When he bent my arm, if he had not had a firm grasp on my biceps, I would have blasted through the roof of the house because of the pain. He further informed me that this had to be repeated ten times each morning and evening. I could hardly believe that a child could endure such pain. He kept reassuring me that unless I endured this physical terrorism, my arm would be frozen at the elbow for the rest of my life, and this left-handed kid didn't want that.

About a week later the number of bends went to fifteen, then twenty, then thirty, always more than the week before. All the while, I could notice a minuscule lessening of the pain from week to week. But one night, with tears of desperation I cried: "But Dad, how long is this supposed to go on?" His reply: "The doctor says <u>**'Until it doesn't hurt so much any more.'**</u>" It's the same with grief work. It's painful, but it pays; it hurts, but it works. That's the way it is with therapy—you continue "until it doesn't hurt so much any more."

For all these past eighty plus years, my left arm has been normal and completely functional. Without the medical attention and the painful therapy, it certainly would have been otherwise. There's no gain without pain.

There are many other things beyond the fifteen I have mentioned which can justifiably be called grief work. **Anything you do that helps is grief work.**

The Bridge

I didn't believe,
Standing on the bank of a river
which was wide and swift,
That I would cross that bridge,
Plaited from thin fragile reeds,

Fastened with bast (fiber).
I walked delicately as a butterfly
And heavily as an elephant.
I walked surely as a dancer
And wavered like a blind man.
I didn't believe that I would cross the bridge.
And now that I am standing on the other side
I don't believe I crossed it.

> Leopold Staff in
> *The Seven Choices* by
> Elizabeth Harper Neeld

If I were writing the poem, the last line would read: "I can hardly believe that I crossed it."

7

Children Grieve Too

Death is a very sure thing in our world. It is understandable that many parents try to protect their children from the discomforts of physical and psychological experiences which might be difficult or traumatic for them. However, in things which have to do with death, the protection and shielding is often overdone. Much of life is made up of things (and people) we gain and lose, and children need to learn early how to face up to loss and work their way through it.

A well-meaning mother found her little daughter's parakeet dead in its cage. Before the child learned of it, she replaced it with a look-alike, because she did not want her child to face the fact that her pet had died. This mother was doing her daughter a disservice, **because any child who is mature enough to love is also mature enough to grieve, face up to the loss, and work her way through it.**

The Big Task

Virginia Satir in her book *People Making* reminds all parents that "children are people with a special way of seeing the world. They have unusual ideas about death, and they are prone to certain misconceptions and difficulties with the subject at different ages. However, children can understand almost anything if it's put to them in the right way. You just have to know the right words to say.

"Parents need to understand the crucial role they play in the future lives of their children after a major loss. Parents teach in the toughest school in the world, the school of making people. In order to help them grow into kind, stable adults we need to listen to them and guide them. We need to treat them like people."

Therese Rando in *Grieving* sums up parental responsibility thus: "Helping children cope with death and mourning is a necessary and difficult but enormously critical task. They have many of the same feelings and needs as you; however, they also have fewer resources and abilities to cope with them."

Many people believe that children do not know anything about death, as the mother of four-year-old Emily said on the death of Emily's grandfather: "I don't think I will tell her anything about her grandfather's death; she's too young to understand anyway. She will be with relatives until after the funeral is over and the family can get itself together again. Then, after she is older, I will tell her." This course of action is the ultimate in ridiculousness!

Our children know more about death than we give them credit for. They see it on television, in the movies, on the newscasts, in the newspaper, in story books, and in song.

But exposure does not equal understanding. Unlike children of earlier generations who normally experienced death in the family at home, very few children of our day have ever actually been close to the reality of death. Consequently, their concept of death may turn out to be bizarre, imagined, fictitious inventions of a child's mind. As a result, the child has to struggle with the very difficult concept of death with little or no frame of reference. In addition, there is a very real contradiction of our times. Death is a terrible thing that threatens all of us everywhere, yet it is not a subject we talk about or even bring up.

Many parents shy away from, or refuse to talk with their children about these things because they themselves have questions about the concept of death which they do not understand, or they are uncomfortable about their own mortality and don't want to talk about it. However, it does no good to sweep the unpleasant subject under the rug and go on with our whistling.

Pet Loss

The loss of a pet affords the child a natural opportunity to learn about death. The child may be encouraged to have a "service" for the pet and bury it, or at least introduce the subject of death by having a simple talk about what happened.

In Nature

The seasonal change of flowers and trees offers another familiar illustration of life vanishing in the winter only to renew itself in the spring. The very small child can comprehend the fact that the dead leaf which has fallen to the ground is all gone now, and it won't come back; it is dead.

Therese Rando in *Grieving* (the most comprehensive and rewarding book I have found on the subject) reminds us that "children do grieve, and most of what is true for adults also holds true in age-appropriate ways for children." While their grief may be like ours, they don't have the words to describe how they feel. Helping them cope is very necessary and difficult, but enormously critical.

It should also be noted that death is not the only thing which children grieve over: Like adults, they grieve whenever they experience a significant loss—when friends move away, when parents divorce, when pets run away or die, when the family has to move to a different community, and even when a favorite toy is lost, broken, or stolen.

You will be helping and guiding your child if you will listen to his or her own version and interpretation of the experience. Children learn important lessons about life through every childhood crisis. But we need to know what they are learning. How the child interprets the events, frustrations and pain of the experience is important, and your child might need some guidance and instruction at this point, because the losses of childhood, if not properly dealt with and worked through, will adversely affect the child for many years to come.

Louise Bates in her introduction to Grollmans' *Explaining Death to Children* makes the statement, which all of us adults have already learned, that **"death is a universal and inevitable process and must be faced."** Loss and grief are a normal part of almost everyone's life. Everything in this world that is alive will someday die. Knowing what death is and learning to face it creatively is one of the most important things we must teach our children, because coming to terms with one's own mortality is a lifelong process, so we should not expect too much from the child. The child needs to understand that "loss and death bring intense feelings which must be dealt with and we must help the child to actively do so (Rando)." If the loss is not handled well, the child may be deeply injured emotionally. In times of crisis, children look to adults for guidance to find out how to act, think, and feel.

Parents play an important part in the maturing of a child's understanding of death when they assure the child that the fabric of family life has not been destroyed. The child needs the assurance that he will be cared for. It is an important insight to understand that life goes on for us after the death of a loved one, or a divorce, or any other major loss. Children need to understand they will not always feel as bad as they do now. They need to learn that "this too shall pass." But it takes patience to work this concept out in our lives. If we don't work it out, unresolved grief can bring about psychological disturbances, adjustment problems, and behavioral disorders not only for children, but for adults as well, and it can and often does last a lifetime.

Statistically, everyone faces the death of someone important to them on the average of once every six years. One child in twenty experiences the loss of a parent during childhood, and nearly all children are confronted with the death of a pet, a neighbor, or grandparents during the early years of life.

Two Important Words

In dealing with a child's grief we must always bear in mind two important words: **UNDERSTANDING** and **COMMUNICATING**.

To be effective in helping the child through loss, we must first understand what degree of maturity the child has attained. We must take into account the child's age and what experiences he or she may have had with death, and unless we know what a child of this age is able to understand, all our efforts to help will fail. We must go where the child is in experience and understanding. Then we need to try to think like a child of that age thinks—and that is not easy, because it has been such a long time ago for us.

The second word is communicating—keeping the doors open by talking and listening. "The most important thing we can do for a grieving child is to talk to him and listen to his observations (Sandra Aldrich in *Living Through The Loss of Someone You Love*)." "It's hard enough to deal with a child when we know what he thinks, but when we don't know what he thinks, it's almost impossible (Dr. David Peretz in *How Do We Tell the Children?* by Schaeffer and Lyons)." This mandates the need for talking things out.

One investigation (Maria Negy) revealed that there are three recurring questions about death on a youngster's mind:

1. What is death?
2. What makes people die?
3. What happens to people when they die? Where do they go?

The answers to these questions comprise a big order. How do we deal with them?

Some Do's

1. First of all, tell the truth in a language the child can understand. When you tell the truth, you don't have to remember what you said when the question comes up again, and it will. We should give answers that will not have to be discarded or unlearned because they were false to begin with, such as in the case of accidental death, suicide, SIDS death, or homicide. If you do not have a real answer, it's okay to say, "I don't know, but I will try to find out." If the child is not satisfied, he might easily let his imagination run wild and come up with something really bizarre, and great harm might be done.

2. Steer clear of contradictory information, be on the alert for misinterpretations or wrong conceptions the child may have about the death, and attempt to clear them up.

3. Avoid the use of euphemisms (substituting a delicate word for one that is offensive). Our death-denying generation speaks of pets being "put to sleep," people "passing away" or "expiring." What we really mean is that they are *dead,* and we should not be afraid to use the right word.

4. Be accepting and open. Never criticize the child if he comes up with a wrong impression or idea.

5. Be positive—your attitude is very important. Children need to learn early in life that bad things do happen to good people. We cannot escape them, but we can learn to live with them; sometimes this learning to live with them might be the closest we can come to a solution or resolution of the loss. If we can succeed on this point, there will be fewer lasting emotional scars. If a wound does not heal, that is not the end of the matter. An open wound may lead to further infection, and that may mar or even ruin the rest of life. Children need help in facing the loss and working their way through their grief.

6. Encourage the child to grieve and give expression to his or her feelings.

7. Give the child the opportunity of attending the funeral.

8. Give the child the chance to meet with and visit someone who is terminally ill and also to attend a funeral service of someone not related to or otherwise significantly attached to the child. This might have been done before the actual death of a loved one. Visit a cemetery with the child, encourage his questions and do your best to answer them.

9. Encourage the child to write a letter to the deceased loved one and draw some pictures. These can be placed in the casket at the viewing time or the funeral.

10. Get outside help from relatives, friends, church, etc.

11. Give lots of hugs and affection.

12. Don't hide your tears; feel free to cry with your child and assure him that he will not always feel as bad as he now does if he deals with his loss correctly and creatively. That should always be the way we meet life's problems.

13. Pray for wisdom.

I am indebted to Bob Deits in *Life After Loss* for the remaining four things adults can do to provide the opportunity for healing that children need after the death of a significant person:

14. "Provide an open and honest atmosphere in which it is easy for children to ask questions and express their own thoughts and feelings.

15. "Understand how children are interpreting their experience with death or a funeral. The fact that you are willing to talk matter-of-factly about these things is reassuring to children.

16. "Give correct and factual information in as simple a way as you can. A useful and helpful statement to a young child (under seven) would be something like this: 'When someone dies, it means their body is no longer working. Their heart has stopped beating and they don't breathe any more. They don't have to eat or sleep. They are never too cold or hot. Nothing hurts. They don't need their body any more, and it means we won't see them again in this world.'

17. "Help children preview what will happen at a viewing, wake, memorial or funeral service. Describe the room, casket, etc. Should children be allowed to touch the body? Yes, if they want to and are prepared ahead of time. 'You may touch (name) if you want to. However, now that his or her body is no longer working, it will feel different: instead of being warm and soft, it will feel cool and sort of hard. It won't hurt (name) if you touch him or her, and it won't hurt you.'"

Keep The Child Close to You

If a child has lost a parent, it is important that the surviving parent, or the immediate caregiver if there is no surviving parent, remain close to the child rather than completely withdraw into a private grief. This will enable the parent or caregiver to continue to show responsibility and, over time, provide a model for working through the pain to find meaning and worth once more.

Many parents make the mistake the thinking that it would be better for the child to be kept at a distance during the preparations for and the conduct of the funeral. Therese Rando in *Grieving* presents the following caution in this regard: "The loss will be worse if your child is sent away to an unfamiliar environment for 'protection' from adults' grief and from the funeral service. This often results in anxiety, since the child is deprived of the secure and predictable world of the family." Ms. Rando says, "When adults try to shelter and protect children, they then turn to their own imaginations, which often produces a worse scenario than the real one. When they don't know much about cemeteries and burials, they are in danger of dreaming up all sorts of conclusions as to what was done with the body, etc. Children need to know about these things, and they need to be shown how to face them. They can handle the truth and the grieving if it is given in doses measured to their capabilities.

The most important thing that we as adults can communicate to children of any age is that life will go on for us after a death, divorce, or other major loss. Some things will never be the same again; we may never get over our loss, but we can get through it and life can go on again. Reassurance is important to children. They need to feel that although the one area is rocky, other areas are stable. Give reassurance that they will continue to be loved and cared for. Balance the negative reality (loss) with positive truth (hopeful future). This can be applied to most crises that children face: Only one area has been touched; everything else is the same. If a child's friend moves away, the child needs to be reminded that this does not end the relationship: "You can write to each other and exchange visits with each other as soon as possible. You can maintain contact."

Most of us, unless our life work is with children (teachers, counselors, pediatricians, etc.), have a difficult time trying to determine what concepts a child can understand at any age. Also, children follow their own timetable in maturing, and they are all different. "Growing up is not something that is done by the calendar or slide rule (Edgar Jackson)." They are not all together in this race. Some are years ahead of their peers, while many are far behind. Age differences which follow in this section are only approximations. Whether the child we are trying to help is ahead or behind the norm is not important. The important thing is to know **where** that particular child is. We may need to ask questions to determine this and then act accordingly.

Loss and grief are a normal part of everyone's life. Because small children perceive death and loss differently, they respond differently than adults or older children do; they express their sadness in ways appropriate to their age and development.

Infancy

The infant's awareness of the world is very narrow. It includes the mother, others in the family, the family pet, and a doll or teddy bear. Its needs are simple: physical contact, love, stroking, warmth, food, dry diapers, and consistency. Probably most children come to understand the meaning of loss or separation during their first year. Infants have no concept of time or death. Most children under four years cannot conceive of someone's going away and never coming back. Even if death is talked about and explained, it doesn't make sense. He sees the bad guy get killed on the television one day, and the next day he's back again, in another story but very much alive. What's a kid to believe, anyway?

The small child has several basic fears: the fear of falling, loud noises, and the fear of being separated or abandoned, all of which may be associated with a separation from the child's source of security. The separation/abandonment syndrome comes into play when a baby-sitter arrives to take over the child for the evening while the parents have the night out. Most infants cry up a real storm during the first few instances. This might also occur when the food does not arrive on time.

Pre-School (Ages 2-6)

Children of this age are too young and inexperienced to comprehend the full meaning of death; they may sense loss, sadness and separation, but they are not too young to respond at their own level. No matter how well we try to explain death, the very small child may still interpret it as a deep but temporary sleep. By the time they enter the first grade, some will have become aware that dying is forever. Most children of this age feel that death comes from an external source, such as a bogey man, a monster, a skeleton, or an angel who takes people away. Many children interpret it as going to sleep or being less alive; that it hurts; that it is catching; or that it can happen because the child wished it on someone. After a death in the family, the child may be afraid of being away from home or out of the parents' sight.

Schaefer and Lyons in *How Do We Tell the Children?* cite two examples of two children's normal reactions to the death of a loved one:

"One researcher in the field of child bereavement described the way a little boy whose brother had died handled his grief in fantasy play: He buried his brother's toys in the sandbox. Gradually the child worked through his grief. His parents had put a picture of the dead child in the boy's room; the family started to talk about how they missed his brother; and finally, one by one, the child removed the toys from the sandbox and put them back on the shelf." It was his way of accepting the death and working his way through his grief.

"Jenny's mother was similarly sensitive to her child's reactions. After her mother had explained the facts, four-year-old Jenny asked when she could see Grandpa again. Her mother explained, 'Not for a long, long time, after you die and get buried and go to heaven.' But Jenny, like many children her age, was persistent. 'Will God make him better and send him back?' 'No,' answered the mother. 'Once a person's body stops working, it won't work any more, and he is dead. He won't come back.' The mother said Jenny accepted that pretty well after she had cried for a while. Then I said, 'No matter what happens, you still have me, and she seemed fine ever since.'" This might be an opportune time to share your family's beliefs about the power and mercy of God. A death in the family is a perfect time to teach a child about faith.

Children adjust more quickly when they feel they're in on things. Parents and other caregivers should speak openly and directly, holding the child's hand as they reassure with words like "I understand; I know how you are feeling; we are all very sad about this. We are going to miss (name) a lot, and sometimes we'll cry about it, which is okay." When the child persists in not accepting, give that child a big, long, strong hug. It might be helpful for us to remember that the major reaction to loss by death for a child of this age, and later, is a fear of what is going to happen to him. Children sometimes experience guilt, feeling that they may have caused the death by wishing the person dead; or anger at the loved one for abandoning them, and a great deal of confusion about what it all means. For us as adults who have weathered many losses, we react to death in many of the same ways, because we have been over the road before, but for a child who has had no experience in this field it must be overwhelming.

Bob Deits in *Life After Loss* tells the story of Anita and the very inappropriate ways her parents dealt with her.

"Anita was four when her grandfather died. When she and her parents arrived at her grandparents' house, her grandfather's body was laid out in a casket in the front room. Anita was told that she must stay in the dining room. She peeked around the corner and saw a room full of adults standing around her grandfather's body. Several were crying because he was dead, but she didn't know what that meant. She wanted him to get up and play with her, but again was told she must stay in the other room.

"On the day of the funeral, Anita was not allowed to attend the funeral, but was taken to the cemetery. When the casket lid was closed and it was lowered into the ground, she began to cry. She couldn't understand why they were leaving Grandpa alone in the ground. She thought he would be lonely and cold in the dark. She wondered if he had been bad and somebody was mad at him. Then it was time to leave, she tried to tell her parents that her grandfather had not kissed her goodbye, but nobody was paying any attention.

"Anita still carried the memory of this sad experience when she became a grandmother herself." Not being given the opportunity to grieve the loss of her grandfather at the time of his death caused her to carry her unresolved grief on into adulthood.

Elementary School Age

During these years, children come to a better understanding of death because they may have lost a pet, friends, or loved ones, but still have developed a minimal capacity to deal with it. They gradually realize that death is the end of life in this world, that it is final and universal and that they too will someday die. But death is no longer a bogey man who catches and carries off his victims, but a biological process. The Swiss psychologist Jean Piaget says children go through stages of distinguishing what is alive and what is dead.

The child probably grasps the concept of death intellectually, but may be having a hard time letting it sink in and may have had little opportunity to share his grief. It is hard for a child of this age to translate ideas into concrete terms. The same questions may be asked over and over again. If a child has lost a parent, one of his greatest fears will be that the other parent might also die. This fear is not limited to small children. Nina Donnelley in *I Never Know What to Say* tells about her assignment to speak to 200 high school youngsters. She could not make up her mind what she should speak about until one day she asked her sixteen-year-old stepdaughter what kids her age were most worried about. The answer stunned her: "The possible death of their parents." She took the cue, made that the main thrust of her speech, and received two standing ovations. It should also be said that even though a child has not suffered a loss by death, this might be the biggest worry of growing up. Even the younger child sees the possibility of this and worries, "Will we have to move? Who will take care of me?"

It is common for children of this age to have feelings of guilt and fear that their own words, thoughts, or wishes might have caused the

death. That's one good reason why no one should ever tell a child of this age, "You'll be the death of me yet."

Parents sometimes become unduly upset by what they interpret as a child's lack of feeling. A small boy had been told of his grandfather's death and had shed some tears upon hearing the news. An hour later he was seen in the back yard playing catch with his best friend. What might have been interpreted as a lack of feeling was in reality the boy's defense against being overwhelmed by his grief. He creatively changed his thought pattern by doing something else so he wouldn't have to be thinking about his loss. This is not a bad idea. Children often work their way through grief through play, a medium for healing with which they are most familiar.

At this age, a child may be cued in on some of the medical details surrounding the death. Sometimes it helps the child to accept the fact. And facts are worth more than fancies. Most children feel that dying is painful, when in fact it's usually more painful for those who are left behind. Then there are some who believe that death is catching, like measles, so it's wise to stay away from a bereaved person.

Losing someone by death makes us feel alone and cut off. Children feel that way, too. This comes home to the bereaved youngster the first day back at school after a death in the family. The wise and caring teacher should prepare the class for this by explaining whatever details surrounding the death she feels are necessary for them to know and encouraging them to act as normal as possible when the bereaved youngster appears and to try to be careful not to say something that would be out of place. Children can sometimes be very cruel in what they say. The teacher should also encourage the children not to tease, ignore, or make any mourning child less a part of the group. The teacher might privately meet with the child and get his own input on what he expects from the class. Would he want them to talk with him about the death, ask questions, etc. If they stand off by themselves and treat him as though he had measles, the bereaved youngster might feel rejected or abandoned by his peers, and this is a hard blow to handle.

Children need to be told what to say and how to act when someone dies. If they are embarrassed or don't know how to behave, they may act silly or laugh; on the other hand, they may become very quiet when they see someone who is grieving. Trying to feel with the child is an important ingredient in helping him deal with his loss.

Most people write letters or send condolence cards to those bereaved, and that is to be encouraged. But if a child has lost a parent or a sibling, in addition to sending the card or letter to the family, also send another, in a separate envelope addressed to the child. The child will never forget your thoughtfulness.

If the child has learned to write, personally present him with a diary and encourage him to write down his thoughts and feelings; he will be helping himself work his way through his grief. The longer we work at it, the less it will hurt, and it won't always hurt as much as it does now.

"In responding to the needs of the young child, the caregiver must provide an emotional sense of comfort, love, warmth, attention, and acceptance. In other words, the process of helping the child cope with the loss demands a 'helping-healing adult who can provide the emotional support and care necessary' (Wolfelt)."

Pre-Teen (Middle School)

During these years, a child's world grows very rapidly, just like his body. His world gets bigger as he gets to know more people. He has new feelings about time and distance. This is often described as the clumsy age. He seems to be neither fish nor fowl. He is no longer as dependent as the small child, but he's also not an adult. Maybe that is why he is called a middler. This is a very difficult but extremely important age for the child. It is the stage during which children are trying to find and establish their own selfhood. Their knowledge and emotional skills are in transition as they move back and forth between childhood and adulthood. Sometimes they may act like a child, while at other times they may appear to act like an adult. Within them a new meaning of love is also emerging.

This is probably the most difficult and frustrating stage in the total process of growing up. The child is beginning to experiment with all kinds of ideas and theories—a very dangerous time, to be sure. Standards and concerns become very important as he develops his own sense of morality, of right and wrong.

Because these years are so filled with change, the child's grief and mourning may go unrecognized, probably because he lacks opportunities to share his grief with others. He has gotten beyond wondering about what death is, even though he may be unable to fully accept its finality. Self-esteem is beginning to grow as we see the many instances of "acting grown up" in an attempt to master the pain of loss and deny his own helplessness. Underneath all this may be a tendency to be fearful of many things and develop phobias of one kind or another.

We should not assume that the child knows the same things an adult knows. That's what parents are for, just as in the animal world the young learn survival skills from the parent; otherwise they would never survive.

One of the finest and most helpful things you can do for a child of this age is to steer him into some research on his own as he grapples with the experience of grieving. In the bibliography at the end of this book, there is a lengthy list of books written for children and parents who are in grief. Your local librarian will be glad to suggest the most popular and helpful ones. Books can provide a catalyst for discussion; you need to talk with your middler and open up dialogue; be there!

The Teen Years

The teen years are exciting years; their bodies are growing so fast; they are rapidly becoming aware of the vastness of the world and the problems which need to be solved; how to relate to something so vast can be bewildering. Powerful sex drives are beginning to emerge, and rather than being excited and thrilled about all this they may evidence a sense of moodiness and ennui. Teenagers exercise philosophical capabilities about life, love, death and society which younger children do not possess. As they move through the teen years, death takes on a social dimension, because they may have experienced the loss of a loved one or friend. This raises philosophical questions about the meaning of life: Why are we here? The world is in such a mess; is there anything we can do about it?

By this time, they are well aware that death is universal, inevitable, final, and irreversible, but in a teen's philosophy teenagers never die; they feel they are immortal. Perhaps it is because they have never really visited a cemetery and noticed the dates on the headstones. People of all ages are buried there.

Some of the most horrible memories I have of funeral services I have performed have been those conducted for and attended mostly by teenagers. There is so much crying, groaning, and feelings of hopelessness and frustration. They believe in death all right, but it's always a long way off. It reminds us of what we've seen on television showing funerals and other tragedies in Third World countries. Their manifestations of grief seem to us to be greatly exaggerated. They really put everything into their mourning!

One of the reasons teenagers have such a problem with the death of a peer is that they have not lived long enough to have built a philosophy of death into their philosophy of life.

For the teens, life is so intense and full of energy that they feel death cannot touch them. Because they feel themselves so indestructible, death represents an intrusion on their sense of reality and it says that teens are not imperishable. This realization can be very painful, and the death of a peer is a special challenge to their sense of security.

Teenagers believe in death, but they also have a fear of it, and in order to conquer their fears and prove that they are immortal they may engage in all sorts of wild and impulsive death-defying behavior, legal or illegal, like reckless driving, or accepting a dare which is life-threatening. They put themselves in situations where they must win over great odds to test their own mortality, and if they win, they have proved that they are invulnerable by gaining control over it.

James T. Clemons, who edited *Sermons on Suicide,* makes the following statement: "A recent study shows that in the normal life cycle of a person, feelings of isolation, loss and stress are never greater than around age sixteen. It is as traumatic as it is normal to move from the securities of childhood to the insecurities of adolescence and adulthood. In the process, one experiences body chemistries heretofore unknown, along with a variety of new feelings and emotions." Anger can sometimes be a big factor. A child may develop ambivalent feelings about the one who died: Why did he leave me? And he remembers unkept promises, etc.

How do we help the teenager? First of all, BE THERE. His situation is much like someone who has never learned to swim, being thrown into a large, deep body of water without a life jacket. He needs help, and one reason we see so many teens dying by their own hand is that no one is helping them work their way through their problems. The second thing we can and must do is LISTEN, and accept them where they are. Don't argue, but rather try to be reasonable in a non-pushy way. Remember how you felt when you were a teen. Finally, encourage him to get into a SUPPORT GROUP for teens. If there isn't one in your area, form one. A school counselor could be a great help and resource in starting such a group and directing other teens into it. What I said in the previous section about doing some independent research on grief also applies to this age and possibly even more so. Besides answering questions, it is also helpful to specify the cause of death (cancer, accident, heart attack, etc.). If they do not know that the loved one died as a result of a specific cause, they may develop a fear of sudden death themselves.

Alan Wolfelt in *Helping Children Cope with Grief* sums up his chapter on this subject with the following:

"In summary, children appear to proceed from little or no understanding of death to the recognition of the concept in the realistic form. While most often states are listed in chronological order, the individual child may well deviate from the specific age range and the particular behavior associated with that age. While evidence does appear for the age-level understanding of children's concepts of death, one needs to keep in mind that development involves much more than simply growing older. Environmental support, behavior, attitudes, responsiveness of adults, self-concept, intelligence, previous experiences with death, and a number of other factors have an important role in the individual child's understanding of death."

Don't underestimate the depth of a child's mourning, but help him get through it, and don't be surprised if your child's way is different from yours. "Children need to know that despite the experiences of sadness and loss, life is still worth living, and there is still much to enjoy, much to be loved, to learn not only that it is all right to cry, but it is all right to laugh again as well (Albertson.)."

In his *Life After Loss,* Bob Deits closes this section of his book with the following: "The most important insight adults can communicate to children of any age is that life goes on after death, divorce, or major loss. To do this you must become more comfortable with your own grief."

In addressing the needs of children of all ages at a time of loss, you will serve them well if you:

1. Offer your acceptance of their feelings and behavior.
2. Listen carefully without being judgmental.
3. Assure them of their security in terms they can understand.
4. Make sure they know they are not to blame for the death.
5. Express your love and care for them in unmistakable ways.
6. Act in ways that elicit trust.
7. Answer all questions with as much honesty as you can.
8. Help them understand that circumstances will not always be the same and they will not always feel as they do now.
9. Provide an atmosphere of stability in the midst of any changes.
10. Actively help the child deal with feelings by "clearly and repeatedly giving him permission, through what you say and do, to deal with his feelings. You must actively help him do so (Rando)."
11. Remember that as a parent you are a chief model, a resource of ideas, and a coach of behavior.
12. Offer your child the reassurance that no one knows the right words to use at such a difficult time.
13. Know that there is no single best way to help children manage painful questions, because each child is unique and different from others.

14. Remember that helping a child manage painful feelings during a crisis presents a special opportunity for parents and caregivers to open doors for positive contact and growth. Children need help in expressing their feelings.

15. Know that the important thing is not so much how, when, or to whom the child expresses feelings, but that he or she does find some way to give expression to what is going on inside. If you as a parent are so completely wiped out because of your grief that you feel incompetent to help your child, PLEASE find some other adult to be there emotionally for him. This could be another family member, teacher, counselor, minister, or special friend. Your child will not think less of you for having shifted this responsibility to another person if you explain your reason. Your child may think more highly of you because he knows you are suffering as much as he is. However, do not take yourself completely off the playing field. Your child should know you will always be there for him—NO MATTER WHAT!

Telling the Child

When death invades a family relationship, very often the adults in the family are so upset and occupied with their loss that they pay little attention to the children and make no effort to explain what has happened, and what is going to happen as a result of the loss: visitation at the funeral home, the funeral, burial, etc. A child should be told immediately instead of hearing it from someone else, in which case she might be more frustrated and wonder why you had not told her. Your child's being able to count on your honesty is important.

To better prepare yourself to tell the child about the death, I would recommend that you secure a copy of Therese Rando's *Grieving,* and begin on page 212, and/or Carol Staudacher's *Beyond Grief,* beginning at page 128. Both these sections are very helpful and complete.

Let us say by way of illustration that Roberta is six years old. Her beloved grandfather has just died. Someone very close to her, like you, her mother, should tell her as soon as possible. Your child deserves the dignity of an adequate and understandable explanation. Don't think for a minute that she is too young to understand death.

This conversation should be held in surroundings familiar to the child, like your home, but not in the child's room or favorite spot, lest the association of sad news should always shroud that room in the future.

This telling session will be so important that it should be in private with no possibility of interruption. Take the telephone off the hook and dial one digit, so it will not ring. Speak in a normal voice; hushed and unnatural whispers might give the child the impression that death is spooky and unreal. Don't rush through it; take your time not only to speak but also to listen to any questions she might have. Occasionally, and when appropriate, hug or touch her to strengthen her feelings of comfort and security. Let her know that you are not going to hide anything from her, but will answer her questions if you can, and if you do not have the answer you will try to find it. Reassure her that she is part of this family and will not be left alone, deserted, or excluded. "We will go through this together."

Remember that Roberta is six years old. Try to recall how you absorbed some of the facts of life when you were that age, and what you understood about death at that time. She has probably experienced some losses in her six years of living: A precious toy had broken and became useless; perhaps a family pet had died and she can remember how she felt. No doubt she had found dead birds or other animals. A child of six years is not too young to learn that in our world all living things eventually die, and that includes us. You have now set the stage for telling her that the same thing has happened to her beloved grandfather.

Remind her that her grandfather had been in less than good health for some time; he had been sick, and the sickness got so bad that his body could not handle it. A broken toy might serve as an illustration here. It just broke down and can't be made to work any more. Now that his body has stopped working, he will not do the things he had done before, like seeing, walking, talking, eating, swallowing, speaking, breathing, moving, or going to the bathroom. He cannot do anything; his body cannot feel anything any more; he will never be sad, mad, or happy. It is like a toy whose battery has worn out and there is no power to do anything. Unlike the toy, we cannot buy a new power source for the body. It must be disposed of. This portion of the telling might involve some fundamental things like embalming, having a viewing, and a funeral, cremation and/or burial. When children ask questions about these things, we should give them answers that they can build on later, rather than ones which will have to be discarded because they were false to begin with.

In talking about sickness with a small child, it must be explained that there are ordinary sicknesses which might not require the services of a doctor or a stay in the hospital and that people do not die from these minor illnesses. Serious illnesses are different in that respect, and you might mention one or two that the child might be familiar with. The distinction between ordinary and serious illness must be made plain or the child will be afraid she is going to die if she contracts a bad cold and has to stay home from school several days or if she comes down with chicken pox or some other less threatening illness.

Accidents also cause death and come without warning to anyone. Hence the necessity of always being careful—the ABCs of staying well. Not all accidents result in death, but when a vital organ of the body is so badly damaged that it cannot be repaired, the whole body will die.

Roberta's mother needs to explain to her that she and the rest of the family are going to feel very sad for a long time. This is normal and natural and is not wrong. These hurting feelings are temporary; they will never go away completely; we will always remember Grandpa, but after we have gotten used to his not being here any more, we won't hurt so much. We don't get over our grieving (and the child should be encouraged and permitted to grieve), but we can get through it; the intensity of grief will diminish; life will go on without Grandpa, except that he will always be remembered.

Sandra Aldrich in *Living Through Loss* adds several other items to the list of things which should be talked about: "Let the child see you hurt; don't be ashamed of your tears. Don't tell the child any more than she can handle. If, in watching her face, you notice that her thoughts are drifting, you have probably gone farther than you needed to go at this point. There is no need to over-explain. Just give concrete, simple facts. Encourage the child to express her feelings and be accepting of them. Let the child talk while you listen. Encourage further communication so that when other questions arise, just to let you know, and you will be there." Later, when a child comes with questions about these matters, no matter how full your hands are with work, put the work down and take up the child and answer her questions.

You will probably be amazed at the many times the same questions will be asked. Children do this to reaffirm a previous answer, or they are just checking to be sure that nothing has changed.

Before this first telling session is completed, something should be said about where the body is: It is being prepared at the funeral home for the viewing (visitation, wake, quiet time) and the burial which will follow in a few days. Depending on how old the child is, you might have to make further explanations regarding the viewing, wake, quiet time, casket or memorial service and burial. This will bring up more questions, which you should deal with as simply and completely as you can.

Most of us do better in stressful situations when we know what to expect. There are two principles of communication which must be borne in mind when we discuss death and grief with a child: First, be clear and honest—information which is untrue or unrealistic will do harm later; second, use age-appropriate words that she can understand.

Some Things Not to Say

We live in a death-denying and a death-defying age. More often than not, when we are called upon to mention someone's death, we substitute a more delicate or pleasing expression in place of the word death, which seems offensive and indelicate. We call this euphemism. We may say someone "has passed away, we lost her, he's gone, he went home to be with God," etc. As adults we know what these terms stand for. Why are we so afraid to say that someone "died"? Euphemisms may be appropriate when we are speaking with adults, but they harbor dangers when we use them with children. We know what the expressions mean, but children may not. They fabricate fantasies because they do not understand what the words mean. Following are some examples of expressions we substitute for death, and why we should not use them when dealing with children:

1. "She just went to sleep." This is downright harmful because the child begins to associate sleep with death and may fight sleep for fear that she may not wake up.
2. "Your mother has gone on a long trip." Of course, this is a lie and in no way suggests finality. It violates the rule that suggests we always tell the child the truth. She may begin to question her mother's love: "Why didn't she take me with her? Why did she leave me? I must have done something which made her angry." A child may become fearful that when anyone takes a journey, they may never return. Later, when she finally finds out that her mother died, you will have some explaining to do.
3. "God took our daddy because he was so young and good. He wanted him Himself." This is an attempt to put the blame on someone else, but raises serious questions about God, such as resentment and anger, in the child's mind. "But I need my dad, too. If God is going around zapping good people, he might get me next." This expression does an immense amount of harm to a grieving child, and the child may begin to feel hostile and angry with God. You don't have to be a child to react this way.
4. "We lost Grandpa today." The child's immediate reaction: "Why don't we go and find him?" A very natural response. One writer tells the story of a recently widowed woman who went shopping in a large

store. When she arrived at the check-out counter, the clerk noticed her painful and disturbed look and asked: "Are you okay? Is anything wrong?" The new widow responded with "I just lost my husband." "Oh, that's no problem. I'll page him." Sometimes it's not only children who do not understand the "more delicate" terms we use. Tell it like it is. If taken at face value, the child might associate all sickness with death.

5. "Grandma died because she was so sick." Earlier I explained about sharing with a small child the difference between ordinary and life-threatening illnesses. Most people get sick many times during a lifetime, but they die only once. The child needs to know that possibly the disease was incurable or that it was the kind of illness that the doctor was powerless to remedy.

6. "Your mother went to heaven." The child's immediate response might be to want to join the mother right away. The child may also want to know, "Why is she buried in the ground—isn't she headed in the wrong direction?" Be careful in giving heaven a specific geographic location.

7. At one time or another, most of us have been guilty of saying to the eldest son (still a teenager or even younger) upon the death of his father: "Now you're going to have to be the man of the house." What an incredible burden to lay upon young and inexperienced shoulders! A recently widowed father shared with a counselor that his ten-year-old daughter (the oldest girl in the family) had, since her mother's death, taken on all the household duties—cooking, cleaning, washing, etc.—and was just wearing herself out trying to keep things going just because someone, following her mother's funeral, had told her, "Now you are the mommy in the house."

The Funeral

No child should be forced to attend the funeral of a loved one. Nor should any child be denied the right to attend the funeral of a loved one. There are some who feel that children should not be at a funeral because the sadness would be too hard to bear.

It depends largely on his age and ability to understand the situation, his relationship with the dead person, and, most importantly, whether he wishes to attend. A child should never be coerced or made to feel guilty if he prefers not to be involved. If he does attend he should be prepared in advance for what he will see and hear. The same reasoning holds true in the matter of visiting a very sick friend or relative.

Nina Donnelley, a hospital chaplain, in her book *I Never Know What to Say,* puts it this way: "A child of any age will be better able to understand death and deal with his own mourning if he has come in contact with death <u>before</u> someone close to him dies. But though we are willing and even eager to teach our children about many problems they may have to face in life, we usually have little or nothing to say to them about death until it happens to someone close to them and then we have to tell them! At this juncture, we are usually in distress ourselves, and not always able to think clearly about how best to approach the tragedy with our children," she says. "Looking back, I realize how wise my mother was when she decided to take me to Mr. Keefer's funeral when I was only six; I can picture parts of the afternoon as if it were happening now."

Mrs. Donnelley tells how her mother prepared her for the funeral of their church friend, Mr. Keefer. Before attending the service, she had explained what death was and that it didn't hurt him to die and that being dead didn't hurt him either, so she did not have to worry about that. She told her about the various parts of the service and what they would be like. She also said that his eyes would be closed as if he were sleeping, but he was not sleeping because he was dead.

After entering the church, they stood looking at Mr. Keefer in his beautiful, shiny black coffin. As they stepped a little closer, her mother asked her if she would like to touch his hand as if she were telling him goodbye, which she did without being forced, with her mother holding her hand throughout. She didn't seem to recall being afraid. She later explained: "Now I know what death looks like."

Children should be exposed to death before it invades their family circle. Having a child attend a funeral of someone not near to them is an excellent idea, and more parents should do it. I know that some people will say this is morbid and unnecessary, but Mrs. Donnelley continues: "Giving a child a minimally threatening experience of death, that of either a person or an animal; being with him for security; and answering any question he may have can later prove to be a great help to him in facing the reality of death if someone he loves should die."

Include the Child

If a member of your family dies, it is important that the children over ten years of age, and maybe even younger, be included in knowing about and even in making the plans for the service. The children have a right and a need to be included, because the knowledge they gain about what is going on will help them heal, and reduce their anxiety. If they are excluded from the plans and the service, they may feel abandoned. Before they make the decision to share or not to share, they should be provided with all the facts—where the service will be held, details in selecting a casket, what cemetery will be used, and how and what will be included in the service. This knowledge can reduce some of the anxiety. After all these things have been shared with the child, he should not be coaxed, condemned, or excluded from other family activities should his response be negative. For most children, it would be a memorable event; for a very few it might be devastating. Proceed with caution.

Let us say, for example, that the father of the children has died. One of the children refuses to have anything to do with making the funeral plans. Children take the short view of life—present gratification or what seems to be the easiest way for them. The dissenter needs to be reminded, gently, that this is the last thing he will be able to do for his father. It's a "one time only" thing, and after the service you will have no chance to go back and do it again. Remind the child that this sharing in the plans and the service will be difficult, but the most satisfying things in life do not come easy. Assure him that he will be free to leave at any time during the service if he wishes to. Sometimes the hard way is the best way. Give the child all the facts you can think of. Let him know what to expect so he won't be frightened. Ordinarily, when proper explanations are given, the child will be more comfortable in participating. Never force a child into this, but sometimes a little gentle arm-twisting might be in order. Give the child some time to think it over.

Once I was preparing a service for a middle-aged man who had died. The widow confided in me that she did not know what to do about their only child, a twelve-year-old boy who wanted to be one of the pallbearers, and she could not bring herself to grant his wish. I suggested to her that it was his way of doing one last thing for his father. So she granted him his wish. At the cemetery, seeing him march at the head of his father's casket brought a flood of tears from most of us who were present.

If there is to be a viewing or wake, the first viewing should be for the members of the family alone, allowing plenty of time to get acquainted with the surroundings, asking questions, etc. Let the children know that it's all right to cry, and it's also okay to put something in the casket: a picture, a letter, a toy, a poem, a flower. In my opinion, a child under three years of age should not be encouraged to go to the casket, but it is important that a child of three or four be taken to the wake and/or funeral of a parent. Unless the child has some memory of this, he may never really believe that the parent is dead. He may remember the event, but not the details.

The Burial

Witnessing the burial rites is very important to the mourner, because it helps place a period at the end of this experience. If even the very small children do not go to the cemetery, they are in danger of fantasizing all kinds of things about what happened to the body; this is an unnecessary risk. Witnessing the evidence that the loved one is gone will give the child a clearer sense of the finality of death. In all these things, specific and complete details about what the child will see should be given ahead of time. If the service is to be held at the funeral home rather than at the church, tell the child what the room is like, the arrangement of the seating, where the family will sit and who will sit next to whom, what we will hear (music, talk, prayers), what we will see (the person in the coffin), and what others might do—sit quietly, cry, etc.

Recently I conducted a funeral for an 82-year-old grandfather. Among those who attended were three great-grandchildren, all under ten years of age. Prior to the service in the mortuary I asked to see the three children and one mother in a side room. This was a first funeral for the children. I explained some things about death and the fact that all living things eventually die, and mentioned some of the things they would witness at the service and the burial. I gave each one a piece of paper and shared with them that many times people place notes, flowers or other objects in the casket before it is closed, and that if they wanted to, they could write Grandpa a note and place it with him in the casket. Incidentally, all three of them did this—I noticed not only printed words but also pictures.

After the committal at the cemetery, the guests departed. As I was leaving I looked back and saw the mother and the eldest girl, Meaghan, at the grave observing the lowering of the casket. I later learned that they stayed until the cover was placed on the vault. Incidentally, this little girl showed more emotion and tears in the mortuary and stayed longer with the family around the casket after the others had left. I am sure this was a very meaningful closure for her.

The approach I have tried to share with you incorporates the generally accepted points of view of the best authorities in the field, but they are not necessarily engraved in granite, because there is always the possibility of finding a child who would be devastated and overwhelmed from attending a wake or a funeral. As I said earlier, no child should be forced into compliance, but neither should a youngster be easily permitted to eliminate the hurdles and the hard places in life just because it's easier that way; later on, taking the easy way may become his pattern of life. The only way through something difficult is to go through it.

8

What Recovery Will and Will Not Mean

What you believe about recovering from grief will in large measure determine what you can reasonably expect. Therese Rando in *Grieving* says that **"total recovery or resolution of mourning, in the sense of completely and permanently finishing it and never being troubled by some measure of loss, is a false goal and usually does not occur."** There is no once-and-for-all closure. The pain may heal, but the loss won't. Life will never be the same as it was before.

All too many survivors delude themselves into believing that their loss was just a bad dream; some day, they say, they will wake up and discover that it didn't happen, it never really occurred at all. We might say: "I'm not going to miss him or her, and life will go on and God is in his heaven and all is right with the world." This just isn't so! No one should ever try to make you believe that this kind of recovery is open to you. People who have been through it know it isn't true.

Discouragement

Many people, after they have walked the grieving road for quite a while, discover that they are discouraged and feel they cannot go on. "I'm not making any progress. I move forward three steps and then slip back two. It just seems that I'm not getting anywhere." In this chapter we are going to be talking about some signs we can see along the way that will help us take stock of our progress or lack of it as we continue to persevere.

Whether you are healthier and happier or weaker and sicker and sadder depends on many things, but mostly on the way you handle your grief and do your grief work. When the work of mourning is finished, the reality of death is accepted. The question is, will you or won't you follow through with the grief work in your search for recovery? Grieving is inevitable, but recovering is not.

Scars

After you have been through the worst of it, you will find that the experience has left you with a scar which marks the place where the miracle of healing has occurred, and we will have to learn to live with it. Maybe that's the best we can hope for. All of us have many emotional scars, but what is the alternative to a scar? If we do not go on to some kind of resolution of our sorrow, we will have an open wound for the rest of our lives, because it was never properly cleansed and it hasn't healed. Unresolved grief can and will last a lifetime.

The lower left corner of the Path chart describes the person who never makes the turn toward recovering: "Resigning yourself to 'poor me'; chronic depression; anger towards self and others; physical, mental and emotional illness; low life satisfactions; unhappiness, and the end result: NO REAL RECOVERY."

There will be times when a scar will ache and throb; maybe we accidentally bump it or we make the wrong move and we are reminded. This is true of emotional as well as physical scars. At such times we need to do something that will enable us to tolerate the pain until it passes: Call someone on the telephone, get out of the house, go for a walk or for a drive, do something nice for yourself or for another, or whatever might help you feel better.

What Recovery Will Mean

The goal of your recovery should be to learn how to live with your loss and adjust your life accordingly. If I'm going to have to go through life with just one leg, I probably would not try to make my living climbing mountains, or doing something that would necessitate my climbing ladders much of the time.

William James, probably the greatest psychologist our country has produced, near the close of his life in 1910 made the statement: "The greatest discovery of my generation is that human beings can alter their lives by altering their attitudes."

Sometimes when a patient is desperately ill and life hangs in the balance, loved ones may ask the doctor, "Will he make it?" and the doctor may reply: "It's up to the patient. If he has a strong will to live and really fights for his life, he may win, but if he has given up, there's nothing any of us can do for him."

The will to live and the willingness to give up are both attitudes over which we have some control. The person who can honestly say, "I'm going to find my way through this" has already won a big part of the battle. You may never get over your grief, but you can get through it. You will never forget the loss of the loved one, but you will no longer be acutely aggrieved and go through the rest of your life crying all the time. Persistence pays off. Endurance and perseverance are the most demanding challenges of finding resolution to the grieving process. Judy Tatelbaum says in *The Courage to Grieve:* "The most basic cause of unsuccessful grieving is our lack of knowledge about experiencing and completing the mourning process," because grief is not an illness that needs to be cured, but an experience which needs to be worked through. We cannot choose what life brings to us, but we can decide what we are going to do with or about it. We have the choice of becoming either bitter or better about our loss. You may already be aware that both of these qualities are attitudes, and can be altered. Some problems in life are unsolvable, but they can be made manageable.

No book or guide or support group or counselor can recover you from your grief. Only you can recover yourself from your grief. The doctor does not recover the sick person. The doctor is merely the facilitator in the process. He helps the body to recover itself. To fight disease he may administer medication aimed at destroying the disease; if there is infection, he will perform the necessary surgery to cleanse the area and provide medication to help it heal. Sometimes he may prescribe a special diet or certain exercises to bring strength to part of the body.

In years past, pneumonia was very often a killer disease. That is no longer true. Most of the people who die of pneumonia in our day are those who suffer from AIDS or are elderly, because today when a doctor has diagnosed a patient as having pneumonia, megadoses of penicillin are administered. In a very short time, it is diffused within the body, adding millions of new germ-fighting organisms to the bloodstream to bolster the depleted and wearied disease-fighting organisms which had become outnumbered and were losing the battle. If the disease is caught early enough, in a matter of hours the tide will turn and the patient will begin to recover. So it is in mourning—we need all the help we can get, and the sooner the better.

Recently, a young lady called me on the telephone and told me of her great loss and wanted to know if attending a Grief Recovery Seminar would help her. Her question was: "Can you take my grief away?" My reply was "No, I cannot take your grief away. It is possible that only God could do that. But we can help you go from a grief which you cannot handle to a grief which you can handle, and life can go on for you again."

Quite often someone gets upset when I keep telling them, "I have good news and bad news for you. The good news is that there is help for your grief; the bad news is that you have to help yourself. No one can do it for you; you have to work your own way through it."

For most of us life is more than just drifting aimlessly through 50, 60, 70, 80 years or more. We have aims and goals—areas which we want to reach, and this takes planning and working. Death rarely enters our thoughts. That is something that always happens to someone else anyway. But when setbacks and disappointments come, we have to steer our way through them. The skipper of the forty-foot fishing boat may sometimes get caught in heavy seas. But he stands resolutely at his wheel and steers the craft, and as a passenger, I'm glad he does. He is aware of the tides and the currents of the sea, the force of the wind as it pushes against his little craft and many other things which contrive to drive him off his course. Success in that kind of venture depends on good navigating, and so it is with life. That's what this book is all about— navigating your way through a loss which threatens to undo you. If I don't succeed in showing you how to do this, I will have wasted my time and you will have wasted your money in purchasing my book.

Grief brings many changes and adjustments, due to changed circumstances in our lives. Just like the skipper of the little fishing boat, we must steer our course in relation to the tides, drifts and other forces which threaten to take us off course. We accept these things in the sense of learning to live with them as inescapable facts of life.

Going it Alone

One of the first hurdles we have to handle is learning to live in a world where the loved one is gone and you have to go on alone. For a woman, one of the greatest changes which comes to her in the loss of her husband is that of her identity. She no longer walks beside a man who will share goals, dreams, and visions with her. She is now alone, bewildered, frightened, and vulnerable. She may still sign her name "Mrs." if she wants to. This is a real identity crisis. With the bereaved husband, much the same thing is true. If there are children in the home, he soon realizes he is both mother and father. He is going to have to learn how to cook, pack school lunches, keep the house clean, do the laundry, and all those other things.

In following these pursuits, the bereaved will be performing items 3 and 4 in the KEY section mentioned earlier: learning to live without the loved one and withdrawing emotional energy once used in dealing with the loved one and reinvesting it in other relationships—a person, object, goals, ideals, and other pursuits.

Changes that come can be positive or negative. You can be richer for the relationship you had with your loved one, or you can be diminished because the death angel came and sliced your life in half and left you with the smaller part. It all depends on how you accept it. Dale Carnegie's advice is appropriate at this point: "Count your blessings, not your burdens." Instead of asking why you had to lose your loved one, be thankful for the years you had together. Emil attended our seminar several years ago after he had lost his wife of forty-seven years. Both of them were great Christian people. Someone in the group one day said that Emil didn't seem to be suffering like so many others. He replied: "I'm just thanking God for the forty-seven years God let me have her." Each one of us must make our decision as to how we are to accept the loss. Like the physical scar, our emotional scars can give us character or be sources of vulnerability.

Many goals will have to be redefined. As was mentioned earlier, we cannot choose what life will bring to us, but we can decide what we are going to do about it.

In my earlier book, *The Mourning After,* I tell the story of the two Oriental weavers: "This principle might best be illustrated by the Oriental story of Jussef and Ahmed, two young men who day after day sat weaving at their looms. Each morning they were given a supply of yarn for the day, brilliantly colored to represent the galaxy of human emotions. One day there was delivered to both of them a large heap of yarn, most of it black, the color representing sorrow. Yussef was discouraged by such a stark color as he wove the yarn into his pattern in harsh patches, wondering all the while how anyone could make something nice out of this. There were gold threads of Happiness, purple threads of Pain, and blue threads of Discouragement. Yussef did not bother to use any of them. The colors he did choose he shot with bitterness into his pattern. Ahmed, on the other hand, used his allotment of black yarn differently as he wove it into his design with understanding sympathy. With bold artistry he skillfully blended his allotment of precious threads with care and tenderness into the pattern as he wove.

"At the end of the day when the master came to inspect their tapestries, Yussef growled that he had not been given the proper yarn. His tapestry was mediocre, almost worthless. But when the Master examined Ahmed's work, he found it a masterpiece of the weaver's art. Ahmed had mingled light with shadow. Then the Master gently said to the two craftsmen, 'Both of you had the same materials and you used them as you wished.' It is not what comes to your life that determines the pattern, but the use you make of it.

"If you react to sorrow in a positive and creative way, it may bring a whole new dimension to our lives. A diamond has many facets, and so has a life. Eyes that have never known tears may lack genuine tenderness. The heart that has never been torn by anguish from the loss of a loved one has never sounded its own depths. Only as grief enters into and becomes blended with other elements of our personalities can we emerge as full and mature persons.

"We grow strong through storm and conflict. Someone has suggested that we never 'are'; we are always 'becoming.' We are the unfinished masters of an unfinished world. After the experience of mourning has run its course, there will be wounds that still ache; there will be losses still hard to bear; but no matter how we may feel about the sorrow itself, most of us would be unwilling to surrender what it has brought and taught us, and we would be reluctant to go back to being the kind of person we were before the sorrow came to us. The softening, hallowing touch of grief leaves its indelible mark upon our personalities."

So in a very real way we decide what our attitude is going to be. Are we going to make it, or even try? Am I going to be better or am I going to be bitter? This is where a therapist can help us. Judy Tatelbaum in her book *You Don't have To Suffer* speaks to this point when she says: "If we are to live as designers (victors) instead of victims of our lives, we must keep generating something to live for. It seems to me that the best testimonial we can give to our dead loved ones is how well we recover and live our lives after a loss, not how much we grieve. We have a choice about how, how much, and how long we grieve." We do not honor our loved ones by dying with them.

The pain clinic is a relatively modern institution on the medical scene. Miracles are wrought every day in these places where therapists, doctors, and counselors work with patients and teach them how to manage pain that is sometimes so strong that medication cannot touch it.

Have you ever thought what it would be like to lose a leg or an arm, or maybe two limbs? Have you ever known anyone who has had this experience? Do you have any idea what a person has to go through and then come out on top and achieve goals they had never dreamed of before their loss? There are thousands of people who have done just that. We meet them most every day, and if we look closely, we notice that their lives are very much on the plus side.

This kind of recovery does not just happen by itself. Mostly it happens because of the help of a good therapist who keeps reminding the person that one doesn't have to be a whole person physically to make something productive of oneself.

I have a friend who lost his right leg from cancer just above the knee—that was more than 20 years ago, and one would never know it except for a slight limp as he walks. At more than seventy years of age, he still puts in a full day's work at manual labor. I think that if such a thing should happen to me, every morning as I had to strap on that prosthesis I'd be tempted to think of some bad words: "Why me? Why did this have to happen to me?" etc. Only through difficult and successful therapy do most people get beyond that stage. The therapist helps us change our attitude about the situation. The prosthetic leg or the cane becomes the friend rather than the enemy of life and success. We can learn a different way of thinking of the loss or impairment and how we feel about it. One of our modern and unknown authors put it this way:

"The Lord may not have planned that this should overtake me,
But He most certainly has permitted it.
Therefore, though it were an attack of the enemy,
By the time it reaches me, it has the Lord's permission,
And therefore all is well. He will make it work together
With all life's experiences for good.
'We know that all things work together for good to them that love God.'"
(Romans 8:28)

Loss—An Opportunity

For centuries religious leaders have pointed out that we should look at loss as an opportunity for personal spiritual development. After all, we do know that muscles grow strong by resisting pressures. All too often well-meaning friends may try to help the grieving person by saying, "God sent this trial to you for your good." That's really not the proper thing to suggest, because the grieving person may not be feeling very good about God right now, and might even be angry with Him. That fact notwithstanding, many people do take this attitude—that God has a reason why He permitted this thing to happen. They have discovered that stumbling blocks can be turned into stepping stones. One woman was heard to say, "If it doesn't kill me, it makes me strong."

The Jews have had a rough time existing in the world ever since they came on the scene. Yet the Old Testament gives evidence of their great faith in a personal God. Existence for them was hard; they always had so much trouble to deal with. Life for them was a continual uphill battle.

They suffered so much. I sometimes wonder if this could be the reason why so many of our doctors, psychiatrists, psychologists, and philosophers are Jewish. Their interest in the healing arts has made its mark on the history of the world. It came from suffering.

In the stage musical *Fiddler on the Roof*, Tevye, the principal character, says much about the troubles of the Jews, God's chosen people. Then at one point he looks toward heaven and says, "God, why don't you choose someone else for a change?" Perhaps the bereaved sometimes have reason to feel this way.

We've always heard that the only things certain in life are death and taxes. We should add a third thing—loss. We live in a society which teaches us how to acquire and hold onto things, people, wealth, influence, position and power, but very little about how we should deal with loss. Eventually we are going to leave all these things behind us. All life is terminal.

When I was taking Latin in high school, we had to translate a story about a very wealthy Roman who had acquired much of this world's goods. He possessed practically everything that money could buy. He had spent a fortune in building the most beautiful and expensive home anyone could dream of. Across the lintel of its front door he placed the word "Linquenda," which means "I shall leave it." Put that label on everything you own, because someday you will leave it. Our society is ill-equipped to help grieving people experience a successful resolution, because we haven't been educated in dealing with loss.

Grievers have always wanted to recover. But many have not wanted it sufficiently to do anything about it, probably because we didn't know what the process was or how we were to deal with it. Judy Tatelbaum in her excellent book *You Don't Have To Suffer* makes the striking statement: "Grieving is inevitable, but recovering is not." Unless we are extremely well adjusted we have to make the decision to recover. When we get to that lowest or turning point noted on the Path chart, some people do not make the turn toward recovery and readjustment.

Mary Jane was a member of one of our seminars several years ago. She had lost her husband in July of that year. At one of our November meetings, four months later, she shared with us: "One day I just made up my mind. My husband is dead, but I am alive; he is gone, but I am here. So I'm going to get on with my life. That is why I am here." And she did get on with her life beautifully.

We may look for help from many sources—support groups, reading good books on the subject, and talking with other people. Basically, our greatest resources are in family, faith, and friends. Find some ideas which sound good to you and try them. Not all things work for all people; we are different and each grief is unique, but most of those who really work at recovering report that each positive action has brought some measure of relief; yet total resolution still seems far away, and the zest for life still has not returned. For most people resolution comes only after many investments of time and energy.

Dr. Elisabeth Kubler-Ross often mentions the stages through which dying patients go: denial, anger, bargaining, depression, and finally acceptance. Grieving patients also go through most of these: we may have to deal with denial that the death has really occurred; we can, and often do, become angry about it; however, it is too late to do any bargaining, because the loss has already occurred. Depression may last a long time, but if we persevere all the way through we will arrive at the point of acceptance—being willing to accept what is, no longer fighting the loss but determining to live with it and get on with our lives.

Following is a list of items which indicate a high degree of recovery. The first seven are suggested by John James and Frank Cherry in *The Grief Recovery Handbook*. The remaining ones have been gathered from other sources.

1. You are feeling better.

2. You are claiming your circumstances rather than their claiming your happiness. You become self-directed, no longer being like a tumbleweed driven by every wind that blows across the desert because it has no motive power of its own. It finally ends up in a corner somewhere, because it had no plans of going anywhere. You are managing your grief instead of its managing you.

3. You find new meaning for living without the fear of future abandonment.

4. You are able to enjoy fond memories without having them bring painful feelings of loss, guilt, regret, and remorse.

5. You can acknowledge that it is okay to feel bad from time to time, and you can talk about those feelings no matter how those around you may resist.

6. You are able to forgive others when they say or do things that you know are based on their lack of knowledge about grief.

7. One day you will realize that your ability to talk about your loss is in fact helping another person to get through his or her loss.

8. You will also find new opportunities and priorities which you formerly overlooked, maybe taking up some pursuit or hobby you began earlier in life but never followed through on.

9. You have become aware again of the loved ones you still have. Many times in a home where a child has died, the siblings feel neglected because Mother is always crying and talking about Jimmie until one of the children finally says: "But, Mommie, you still have us and we still need you. No matter what you do, you can't help Jimmie, but we are here and you can help us."

10. You are committing yourself to living more fully and meaningfully.

11. You are gaining a new and increased awareness of the precariousness of life and its brevity.

12. You are learning not to put off the important things you can say and do today. You have learned to enable your loved ones to smell the flowers while they are still alive.

13. You have become aware of any unfinished business you might have with those who are close to you while they are still with you.

14. You are enjoying an increased family commitment and unity.

15. You have developed a greater personal growth and an increased interest in spiritual things.

16. You can see an increase in your productivity because you are using your loss to transform your pain through art, literature, music, writing, and other creative efforts. In this way you are transforming your pain and rage into getting something done. Mothers Against Drunk Drivers (MADD) was formed by a mother whose child was killed by a drunk driver. This mother's effort and the organization she established have increased the awareness of all of us in this problem and have helped us make our world a safer place in which to live. Whenever we reach out to help others who may be worse off than we are, we are in reality translating our despair into compassionate hope and love.

17. You are becoming increasingly aware of your new identity. Once you have gotten through the grieving and are moving your life in the right direction, you will be different in ways you never dreamed of. You will be more concerned, compassionate and capable of intimacy, and more able to deal with the changes of life.

18. When you imagine that the person you have lost seems to be moving farther into your memory, it's a sign that you have been climbing the steps of mourning successfully.

Perhaps the list of positive things I have mentioned has gotten too long. It might take the greater part of the rest of your life to achieve all of them, but several years down the road you will be able to look back and see how far you have come, because after you have worked your way through most of it you can say to the world, "I have been to the mountain, and I have survived. Now I can handle most anything life brings to me." Within yourself you might be saying, "I never thought I could do it, but I did it." You will have changed—for the better.

Of course, there is a flip side to all of the above—you can become hardened, embittered, cold, closed, and unwilling to reach out for yourself or to others. The choice is yours.

Many people who walk the grieving path never have to make a decision about getting through it. They are so well adjusted to life that everyone who knows them realizes they will get through it, and they do. That's just the way they have handled all of life's difficulties. They face life head-on and no one worries about them. They are like the unsinkable Molly Brown; they are a joy to know and an inspiration as a friend. No matter what, their word is always UP.

On the other hand, there are some people who never get over to the recovery side. They don't want to work their way through grief sufficiently to do anything about it. One day I called a man who had recently lost his wife. I invited him to our Grief Recovery Seminar. He adamantly informed me that no one could help anyone else get through their grief. "So I'm just going to stay home and forget about it." This poor man and so many others who think like he does continue crying all the way down the grieving road and go on living in the area of the last line: NO REAL RECOVERY!

What Recovery Will Not Mean

I repeat what I said in the beginning of this chapter: that total resolution of grief is a false goal and usually does not occur.

Recovery will not mean that you will forget your loved one, because living without recollection is, in a sense, betrayal. Memories will be with us as long as we live.

Recovering does not mean that you will no longer have relationships with your loved one. How can one have relations with someone who is dead? "I buried him; I know where his body is." Most widowed people when faced with a big decision will ask themselves the question: "What would he or she do in this situation?" We have relations with them when we talk with them, even though we know they are not present and will not answer. This is not abnormal when kept within reasonable limits. We must always remember that the person is dead.

A lady in one of our groups told us of a birthday party she held for her husband, who had died two years before. She invited close friends in;

served all his favorite foods; played his favorite music on the stereo, etc. She reported that it was a great success.

Most of us have remembrances of this sort at the point of a birthday or anniversary. We may take flowers to the grave or have a dedicated bouquet at our church on the Sunday near a special date. These actions can be very comforting and beneficial.

Recovering does not mean that you are always going to be happy and never experience pain. You will never forget, and remembering often brings pain.

When we say you will recover, it does not mean that you will not experience the bittersweet combination of feelings that holidays bring, as you rejoice with those still present and inwardly mourn and long for those who are no longer here.

Recovering does not mean you will not be touched by certain reminders, songs, smells, special locations you lovingly shared together.

Recovering does not mean that at certain events you will not painfully wish for your loved one to be alive and present, and share in your joy and be proud of you. An elderly man was retiring after having served his company many years. They gave him a banquet, presents, and said many nice things about him. When he made his acceptance speech, he thanked them all for being there and said his only regret was that his wife of more than 50 years was not present to share the joy with him because she had passed away a few months ago, "and now I have no one to share these good things with."

Recovering will not mean that you won't mourn any more. Yes, you will mourn, but not acutely. You will learn to live with the mourning in ways that do not interfere with healthy functioning in the new life you now live without the loved one.

In her book *Grieving*, Therese Rando closes her chapter on this subject with a quotation from psychiatrist Gerald Caplan, discussing widows; it can be applied equally to other bereaved people:

"In our earlier formulations we had thought that a bereaved person 'recovers' at the end of the four to six weeks of her bereavement crisis on condition that she manages to accomplish her 'grief work' adequately. We believed that thereafter she would be psychologically competent to carry on with the tasks of ordinary living, subject only to the practical readjustments demanded by her new social roles. During the turmoil and struggles of the first one to three years, most bereaved persons generally learn how to circumscribe and segregate this mourning within their mental economy and how to continue living despite its burden. After this time, they are no longer actively mourning, but their loss remains a part of them, and now and again they are caught up in a resurgence of feelings of grief. This happens with decreasing frequency as time goes on, but never ceases entirely (Caplan, 1974, viii)." You are not perpetually grieving because you have become a survivor.

Therese Rando says, "Most bereaved individuals eventually come to terms with their grief and carry on with their lives in healthy and productive ways. However, total resolution of mourning, in the sense of completely and permanently finishing it and never being touched again by some element of the loss, usually never occurs." Ann Landers once said in one of her columns: "Total recovery may never come. But what you kindle of the ashes of your tragedy is up to you."

One of the greatest and most encouraging statements I have ever seen was made by Ann Kaiser Stearns in *Living Through Personal Crisis*. I share it with you in the hope that you will memorize it and perhaps even make a poster of it to hang on one of the walls of your home:

"Certain circumstances are so overwhelmingly difficult that the best we can do to promote our eventual healing is to mark time, stay alive, and bear up under the worst of our suffering."

"TCF" of Fort Smith, Arkansas, said this in *Heartbeat Newsletter:* "Grief work is like winding a ball of string. You start with an end and wind and wind, then the ball slips through your fingers and rolls across the floor, some of the work is undone, but not all. You pick it up and start over again, but never do you have to begin again at the beginning of the string. The ball never completely unwinds; you've made some progress."

No directions on a recipe card ever baked a cake. You have to take the time and effort to gather the ingredients and put it together yourself.

No road map of our beautiful country ever took anyone on a journey to any of the interesting and exciting places listed there. You have to decide where you want to go, make your plans, set your schedule, get the car ready, then follow through and go.

No architect's drawings or blueprints will ever build the lovely home you have dreamed about. You have to purchase the lot, secure the financing, find a contractor, and then your dream comes true—you build the house.

We have talked only about the most important aspects of grief work. These are primary and fundamental—there are many more. Anything we do that helps us, even in a small way, to pick up the pieces after a great loss is part of grief work. All of it is work you have to do for yourself, and the more diligently and consistently you work at it the more completely and quickly you will recover.

Recovery is not linear. It does not move onward and upward in a straight line, but is zigzagged. Life is never going to be the same again, but life can go on and you can go with it. We do not honor the dead by dying with them. A person wearing a prosthesis may have many reminders to curse it, but it need not greatly impair his or her usefulness. You may want to dig a hole as deep as you want and crawl into it, or you may choose to dig your way out and get on with life. Isn't that what your loved one would want you to do? Mourning is finished when a person can reinvest his or her emotions back into life and in the living.

Forty-five years after the close of World War II, my wife and I traveled to Germany—the place of our roots. When we came to Munich, we were told by the guide that at the close of the war the city had been 60 percent leveled by bombings. But nowhere did we see any evidences of that destruction. Nowhere did we see a brick or stone chimney piercing the sky, standing alone. No piles of rubble. The Germans are proud of what they have. They got to work and rebuilt their city, brick by brick, stone by stone. It didn't just happen. They made it happen.

If you are willing to work your way, there is an end to sorrow. The journey will hurt, but it works; it will be painful, but it pays. Where will you make your investment—an ulcer, heart problems, a nervous breakdown, or will it be in the kind of healing that will help make your life whole again? You will find that when you have done everything you know you need to do, God will add His blessing to your work and you will be better.

It is my hope that you will take to heart the things we have talked about in these pages and apply yourself diligently to work at them so that the experience described in the following poem by Christopher Logue will be yours.

> Come to the edge.
> We might fall.
> Come to the edge.
> It's too high!
> COME TO THE EDGE!
> And they came,
> and He pushed,
> and they flew.

9

Remarriage—Is It for Me?

One of the earliest books written specifically for widows was *Widows—Wise and Otherwise* by Gladys Shultz. The author makes this statement: **"If you are fed up with being a widow, do something—get married. Then you won't be a widow any more. But the last state may be worse than the first."** That is something we need to think about. Because there are a great many things in the world worse than living alone, like living with someone you got teamed with and you just can't stand it!

There are reasons for considering remarriage. I don't expect everyone to agree with me on these things, but I know there are people who believe that when you are married, you are married forever. There will never be anyone else to take the place of the loved one who was taken from you. I have known a number of widows who made this decision and stuck by it, or maybe were stuck with it. I also know a great many widows who are complete within themselves. They have been out in the world a long time; they did most of the things well in working through their loss. Their lives are completely fulfilled. They have gained a new image for themselves. They are more capable than they were before. They have been able to handle the estate their husbands left them. Some even know something about their car, so that the mechanic won't be able to rip them off every time they bring their car into the service station or garage.

I know one widow who is this kind of person. One Sunday morning she arrived home from church and found the paramedics working over her husband on the front lawn. He had suffered a massive heart attack. He died before they could get him to a hospital. She was left with two small children. Because she is a self-propelled woman who always seemed to make the right decision, she took a course in selling real estate and did very well with it for many years. She is extremely involved in cultural and philanthropic things in her city: the symphony, the library, and other philanthropic enterprises. During these years she has been completely busy. She has held every office in her church that a woman could hold. One day her pastor, who was one of her closest and best friends, said to her several years after she had been widowed: "Gertrude, many times I have seen you sitting in the congregation alongside an eligible single man; some of them are wealthy and could make life much easier for you. Have you ever thought seriously about marrying again?" She replied: "No. I've thought about it, but I know that when the one comes along who is right for me and the chemistry is right I will marry him, but not before." She is still in circulation and unmarried, but completely wrapped up in and occupied with the many interests she has. She is completely fulfilled in her own right. A woman in such a situation doesn't need to marry. Her life is completely fulfilled without a husband. She has raised her two children and sent them to college; they have both married and made her a grandmother. She has chosen that route for herself. Some women are built this way; they have everything together and will find their way through it. We admire a woman like this.

There are some things worse than living alone. **It's okay to make mistakes; just don't marry one.**

There are some good reasons for considering remarriage: Some women have a great need for the security of having a man in the house. Why should a woman have to make her own way? Maybe the house is too large and the mortgage too big for you to handle alone. Your husband may have left you with a big mortgage and little life insurance to cover it. Financial reasons for remarriage may be very strong and seemingly insurmountable. Take at least a year or two to consider your options about selling the house. If you really have to sell it, that is a strong reason for doing it.

Many widows have a strong need for companionship and love. Let us say that you had a good marriage; you liked it and you want more of it. No one can tell you not to try again. Many women find that being married to a dead husband doesn't work. Of course, you have your memories to live with the rest of your life, but doesn't it seem more reasonable to get out and have some new experiences so you will have more current memories? You cannot obliterate your memories, but you can record over them in the same way you record a new message over the one previously recorded on an audio tape. There comes a time when you should close the door and move on. The marriage ceremony says, "Until death do us part." That's what happened to you. The marriage relationship has been fulfilled. It's over. You did everything for him while he was alive, but now he's dead, and what more can you do for him?

Of course, I need to tell you that when you start thinking in this direction, you will experience some guilt feelings about being untrue to him. That is natural and should be expected. You have fulfilled your part of the contract. How you live your life from here on is your business; whatever you do with it is up to you.

Some years ago a friend of mine, a successful businessman in our town, died of a heart attack. His widow was almost like the widow I heard of who went about the house shouting, "I'll not have you dead; I'll not have you dead." This man's widow went to the cemetery several times every week. She always came away completely washed out. She was overdoing her allegiance to her dead husband. She was not adjusting to her loss. She came to me asking for help, which I tried to give her. My first suggestion was for her to cut down the frequency of her visits to the cemetery, which she didn't do. She spurned other suggestions I made. After months of this I had decided to cut off the counseling relationship, because she was not getting anywhere and I felt I was wasting my time. But before I had actually said these things, when I walked into her home one day the first thing she said was: "I buried Jim last week." I gave my approval by saying "I think it was about time." She had turned a corner by accepting his passing.

Several months later she struck up a relationship with a widower who lived a few doors away in their mobile home park. A little more than a year later they were married. She had closed the door so she could move on. You will never enjoy the beauty of life on yonder shore unless you are willing to leave the shore you are now on. Now, after more than a decade, she has been enjoying being married again, and her life is going on. She still has memories of her first husband, but she now has ten years of new memories made by experiences with her second husband.

Several years ago, a man and a woman in my group looked across the room one day and something clicked. They began getting better acquainted, doing lots of things together including going on cruises. Their relationship seemed promising, and all of us enjoyed watching its progress. Then one day, in the way that good love stories should proceed, they got married. They each owned a home and had grown children. They did not go to an attorney and have a marriage contract drawn up, nor did they go to any counselor for advice. After all, they were mature adults and didn't need that sort of thing. But they made one tragic mistake: They moved into his home and rented hers to someone else. If financial considerations did not preclude it, they should have sold both homes and purchased another together. In doing that there would be no memories associated with the house they lived in.

There are other ways of handling this sort of thing. Circumstances always alter cases. Now, let's say I had been the man and had known her first husband very well, and we were fishing buddies and had done many things together. I knew he was neither a saint nor an angel, so she could not get away with making verbal comparisons. His presence in her memories would be no threat to me. I could go out in the garage and use his tools, because he was my friend. Now, if I didn't know him and I was constantly hearing about what an angel he was, that would be threatening to our relationship.

With the couple mentioned above, it was his house and most of the furnishings were his. This man apparently did not know that many women are married to their house as well as to their husband. They could have moved into her home, but he would have had to make some adjustments in his attitudes about her first husband, whom he had never met. If you get to the point where you want to share your life with another person, you are going to have to close the door to the past relationship and learn to change your attitudes. Unfortunately, within a year this couple were in the divorce court; it didn't need to happen this way. Their beautiful relationship was destroyed.

The big question which needs to be answered is: Am I willing to be, and interested in, devoting myself permanently to another person and letting that other person completely devote himself to me? Until I can answer "yes" to that question, I should not think seriously about remarriage at all.

I believe that men make mistakes in this area more than women do, because women have deep feelings, and they go very much on what their feelings are. The newly widowed man doesn't like cooking, making the beds, keeping the house clean, and getting the children off to school. Too often the first woman who looks capable and appears willing to enter this situation will be proposed to. The statistics indicate that a marriage entered into for these reasons, and within eighteen months of the death of a spouse, will dissolve more quickly than a normal marriage which had none of these extenuating circumstances. It just happens that way. If you really want to get married just for the sake of being married, if you can't stand living with yourself any more, it's fairly easy to find somebody. But if you want a man who will really fill up your life and make you whole, that's not easy at all; in fact, it's almost impossible. In other words, take the long look. But if you are hard-shelled and you know there can never be another love in your life, then be honest with yourself and with those who are concerned about your well-being and who are trying to get you to meet some eligible and marriageable persons. However, I would suggest that you never say "never." You might change your mind someday and wish you hadn't said that.

I heard one woman say, "I won't ever marry again. No one I know would measure up to my first husband. Why settle for the mediocre when I had the best? I'd rather stay single." And she certainly should, if that's the way she really feels. We should remember that there are many beautiful and precious stones lying out there on the beach. You did not pick up the only one that was there. We have a strange and beautiful way of dealing with our dead: We beatify them when they die; we make saints of them, forgetting that they were normal human beings who didn't always do everything right. They made mistakes, as every one of us does. They had their little idiosyncrasies that bugged us at times. But we remember the things we choose to remember. Shakespeare in *Julius Caesar* made the statement: "The evil that men do lives after them; the good is often interred with their bones." It is equally true that "the good that men do lives after them; the bad is often interred with their bones." And when it was someone we truly loved, we choose to remember the good.

Some of us may go all the way through life without ever admitting to ourselves or anyone else that we have experienced moods of hatred or resentment toward our loved one. As a result of such an attitude, we may spend much time in our efforts to adjust to our loss by glorifying and idealizing by thought and word the qualities of the departed. In this way we unconsciously attempt to resolve the existing guilt feelings. We might say that such purging is our way of paying off an emotional debt. There is nothing wrong with this; it's merely facing up to the fact that our loved one was human, and humans are not perfect. It is wise to review the unpleasant as well as the pleasant relationships with the deceased loved one. It is entirely proper for us to express our feelings in a legitimate and wholesome manner in every dimension of our lives.

If and when the time comes that you become involved with another person and you are seriously considering remarriage, please perform the following exercise: In a kind and loving way tell your intended all the good things you remember about your husband. Really build him up, but don't forget to include a few things about him that really irritated you. <u>Then don't ever mention these things to your intended again, even when you are angry with him.</u> Following this encounter, one of two things might happen: (1) Your relationship with this person will dissolve, because you will have made it plain that no one could ever measure up to your first husband. You are playing with stakes that are too high. (2) Your relationship will be strengthened, because you will have portrayed your first husband as a human being who made mistakes like other human beings do. Most men are not afraid to get into the ring against another man, even a dead one, so long as they know what the competition is. Most suitors would be willing to give it a try.

The statistics for remarriage for the widow are not very encouraging. At age 30, 403 out of a thousand remarry; at age 40 it's 183 per thousand; at age 50 it's 86, and at age 60 it's 46 per thousand. But you are not a statistic; you are a human being, and as such you can do most anything you set your mind to do.

If you are planning a fishing trip and you really want to bring some fish home, the first thing you need to know is where the fish are and then go to that place. Where do you find people who are eligible for marriage? First of all, we should mention grief support or recovery groups. Of course, most of the people in such a setting really aren't thinking about marriage at this point. But you never know. Not infrequently, two people look across the room and see someone who looks like an interesting person whom they would like to know better. That's a good place to start, with perhaps a lunch or dinner date, movie, play, or whatever. Just make sure that at this point in time there should be no commitment; that can come later. There's nothing wrong with two eligible and lonely people doing some things together so they can get to know each other better. I have seen it happen many times in my groups. If you are looking for someone with good character, high ideals, etc., a church is a better place than a bar to find someone with these qualities. Most any city or town of any size at all has singles groups and Parents Without Partners. Watch the newspaper for announcements of their meetings; when you decide that you'd like to look this field over, invite a friend in your same situation to go with you. How are you going to know if you don't really try? If you try, something good might happen—or something bad might happen. If you don't try, nothing will happen.

There's an old Chinese proverb which says, "If you want to feed a hungry man for a day, give him a fish. But if you want him to eat every day for the rest of his life, teach him how to fish." There's a very old fish story most of us learned when we were very small children. It's about Simple Simon who "went a fishing for to catch a whale, but all the water that he had was in his mother's pail." Anyone should know you don't find whales in a bucket. If you are a woman, it would be counterproductive to look for an eligible man in a senior ladies' home, and by the same token a man would not be searching in a retired men's facility.

A woman could enroll in a college class or trade school where most of the learners would be men. This is not a problem nowadays, because the world has now found out that virtually anything a man can do, a woman can do—and sometimes better. If you get into such a group, take every opportunity to ask questions about "How do you do this?" of those in whom you might be interested. If he's a normal man, he will delight in telling most everything you want to know, and if you are a good listener and apt pupil and look into his eyes as he tells you, he might tell you more about some other things you didn't ask about. The possibilities are tremendous! <u>Caution:</u> Before you get carried away with this, you might check the jewelry he wears. If he wears a wedding band on the ring finger of his left hand, you can assume he is married. It's not open season for this kind of man. You don't want to be a home-wrecker.

If you are of senior age, you should become active in a senior center in your area. These helpful organizations provide entertainment of all sorts, like movies, cultural events, arts, crafts, square dancing, etc. Senior centers are good places to look, but you have to go there; they won't come to you.

My friend Gretchen had lost her husband. She lived in a mobile home park, as did her sister, who was also a widow. One day she shocked her sister by asking, "Is there any place around here where we could go and meet eligible single men?" Looking like she had been struck by a bolt of lightning, her sister queried: "You don't mean that you would go out looking for a husband?" Gretchen responded, "Why shouldn't I? I have just had enough of this loneliness. I don't expect some Prince Charming to come and knock on my door and say, 'Here I am; look at me.' I'm going to go out and look for him." Those who seek will find, and she did, and she married him, and she wasn't lonely any more. It was a good marriage.

It's very easy to find eligible single men and women, but finding the *right* one might take a little longer.

Sometimes great things come from small beginnings. As a matter of fact, most all great things started small. Example: One day Susan, a widow in my group, called me and asked what I knew about Bob, a widower in the group. I told her what little I knew and asked her why she wanted to know. "Because he asked me to go to dinner with him Sunday. I'm all up in the air and scared to death," was her reply. She had been a widow for about five years, and he was widowed about three years. I said, "What do you have to lose? You will get a good meal at a nice restaurant and he will pick up the tab. But please remember, you make no commitment for anything in the future at this time." She accepted and acted upon my counsel, and things got off to a running start. Less than a year after that, it was my pleasure to hitch them up in double harness.

As of this date, they have enjoyed almost seven years of a very compatible and happy marriage.

Many years ago, Adeline McConnell and Barbara Anderson collaborated in writing the book *Single After Fifty*. It has long since gone out of print, but your local public library might have a copy. By all means, if you can find it, get it and study it. Chapter 8 has an excellent treatment of "What Men Find Attractive in Women" and Chapter 15 is "So You Think You Want To Get Married—How Do You Know?"

In Chapter 8 of that book, the authors tell us what men find interesting in a woman that makes them want to take a second look: She has a reasonably nice figure; she's trim and neat, well groomed. Men note the exterior first, and there's nothing wrong with that. She is happy; she lives life to the hilt; she has a good attitude and does not try to act as though she were 20—no miniskirt or leotards. After the first look, the man notices understanding, love, compassion and consideration. These are good qualities for any age; many of them should become well polished as we advance in years. It was the Oscar-winning actress Marie Dressler who said: "It is not how old you are, but how you are old." Women who have yielded gracefully to the years and have exchanged cuteness for graciousness and dignity, and have learned to give warmth and understanding, are likely to find opportunities for suitable second marriages.

Now let's look at the other side of the equation—what do women look for in a man? It might sound facetious to hear a mature woman say, "Gray hair just turns me on," but some women are impressed by it. Of course, this is only a surface sort of thing, and any man can have gray hair if he really wants it—that is, if he has any hair at all. Probably the most important thing a woman looks for is security. Most of us have been brought up with the idea that the man is the breadwinner and provider. The young man's life is full of rage and fury of the chase as he tries to get somewhere in the world. The mature man has already gotten there and has the comfortable security that goes with maturity. He is considerate and compassionate. He has a good self-image and wholesome sense of humor. He is a good listener. He wants to know about you (the most important person in the world), and your family and where you've been all these years. He looks into your eyes as you tell him these things. He has good manners—he always opens the car door for you and he carries the groceries into the house. He knows how to fix things around the house and he isn't pushy about sex. He is not coarse or aggressive. He keeps his pot belly in check so he can see that his shoes have been shined when he takes you somewhere.

All these things add up to a challenge, and might even remind you of something you read in I Corinthians, Chapter 13. Do you really have this kind of love? These are qualities which most of us can develop if we really try.

I understand that our word widow is related to the Latin word "vidua," which means empty. I don't have to tell you that emptiness is what widowhood is all about.

As mentioned earlier, William James is remembered as the father of American psychology. He died in 1910. During his lifetime he performed many experiments with animals as well as with human beings. Somewhere in his writings he tells the story of an old man and his faithful dog. They hardly went anywhere without each other. The dog was always at his feet, and he slept at the foot of his bed. One day the man died. In less than a week the dog was found dead at the foot of his master's bed. His reason for living had been taken away. Animals grieve, too.

James also studied the psychology of the grayling goose. This goose, as do many other creatures, mates for life. If her gander should die, strange things automatically happen with the flock. The widowed goose is looked down upon because she is now alone; she has no mate to protect her and provide for her. She is helpless, bankrupt; she is pecked at. At the feeding trough, she is crowded out. Everyone else comes first and she is pushed away. She is no longer accepted as she once was. Eventually she becomes so malnourished and weak that she just wanders away and eventually dies or becomes the victim of a predator. For some unknown reason, the possibility of taking another mate is not in her genes. She does not know what to do to fill up the emptiness of her life.

What happens to the widowed grayling goose closely resembles the experience of the widow of our species. The great difference is that we can know what to do when tragedy and disappointment overtake us. We are not grayling geese. It is a tribute to a lost mate that we should feel that the emptiness within us is so great that we should attempt to fill it as soon as possible. Remarriage is one way of filling that emptiness, but it's not the only way. What works for one person may not work for someone else. <u>Caution:</u> It takes time to work these things out. To rush into a new relationship without looking over the terrain and its implications might bring more tragedy, heartache, and emptiness.

Some Don'ts:

1. Many widows have a big problem with the word "widow." You just hate the idea it connotes. Well, you don't have to use it. Instead you

may say, "I am a single woman" or "I am an unmarried woman." You should not even think of yourself as a widow if it keeps you from looking ahead in a wholesome manner.

2. Don't make any early commitment to a new love. You might want to back out of it later. Take your time.
3. Don't be too independent—a man needs to feel he is needed.
4. Don't talk about your widowhood and the fatigue which accompanies it.
5. Don't marry for money—it might prove to be the hardest way you have ever known of making a living.
6. Don't put chains over every doorway into your life—be open, or no one may ever come in.
7. Don't marry just because you are lonely; buying a loving pet might be a suitable investment, and much less expensive.
8. Don't be over-eager—men shy away from predatory females.
9. Don't sign over any real estate, business, or possessions without first getting legal counsel. Make a marriage contract.
10. Don't marry too soon. One survey showed that most widowers remarry within 18 months of their loss. More than half of these unions end in divorce or abandonment within two years. Take two to four years to get to know each other well; there won't be so many unpleasant surprises that way.
11. Don't live in either his or your home. I realize that sometimes there are extenuating circumstances which cannot be overcome. The better way is to compromise; sell both homes and purchase another together. Then it becomes "our" home. However, should you agree to move into his home, this ceremony should occur: After he has carried you over the threshold and planted your feet on the floor, he should look into your eyes and say: "This is now our home. There is no spirit of any departed person that lives here." And you should say the same to him if you will be living in your home. (You need not carry him across the threshold.)
12. Don't keep comparing your new mate with the previous one. Of course, I know this is next to impossible, but keep your comparisons to yourself and let no word of them escape your lips. Give your new mate a fair chance—emphasize the good you find in him, and don't fail to tell him about it.
13. Don't express your likes and dislikes too much. Be resilient and flexible.
14. Don't marry someone who will not fit into your circle of friends.
15. Don't play hard to get; you might get left, like the one single lady

who waited months and years on the dock for her ship to come in. There was never any ship that looked like the one she wanted. She stayed there so long that the pier collapsed and all was lost.

Some Do's

1. Before you marry again, get rid of the excess baggage of the old relationship. If you don't, it will only get between you and your new love and cause trouble.
2. Make a complete disclosure of any serious or life-threatening medical problems. Your prospective new mate has the right to know these things. Knowing will probably not make your new love change his or her mind about marriage. After all, all of us are terminal; we are all living on death row. No one has any guarantee about how long they will live. I know a mature couple, both widowed, who married even though he was ten years her senior. At one point in their discussion about marriage, he told her: "I don't come with a 90-day warranty, you know." Who does? That was more than ten years ago, and they have had ten happy and satisfying years together.
3. Be willing to make adjustments to your new mate. People who marry young can handle adjustments much easier than older folks can. After having lived alone, it's really difficult to live peaceably with someone else. We do get set in our ways. Whenever I am called upon to perform a wedding ceremony for a couple who are over 50, I go into a discussion of this in the prenuptial conference: "You're not kids any more."
4. If you are planning to marry someone who has children under 18 who will be living in your home, do some research on what it takes to raise someone else's children. Check out some of the books mentioned in the *Remarriage* section of the bibliography at the end of this book. Always agree on discipline, and the child's parent should administer it. Brenda Maddox' *The Half Parent* is a gem on this subject. Your public library might find a copy for you. There are few problems that have no solution!
5. Remember that there is nothing that life can bring to you that you can't handle if you will both really work at it.
6. Count the blessings you find in your new mate; this is better arithmetic than comparing him or her with your previous mate. Emphasize the good.
7. Remember that new things do not always work as they should at the start. A new car may make many trips to the dealer for adjustments,

etc. Every adjustment is a challenge, but if you make enough of them you might be surprised at how well you've done. Sometimes the best solution is to learn how to live with the problem.

8. Pay compliments when they are deserved. Each of us likes to know how he or she is doing.

9. Be willing to do anything to help, and unwilling to do anything that will hinder, the development of a beautiful relationship. This is the secret behind most successful marriages.

If you need further suggestions as to where to look for eligible members of the other sex, here are a few which might prove helpful: Computer dating services—if you go this route and find someone and remarry, and if that marriage doesn't work out, you could always blame the failure on "incomputability." Look up a teenage sweetheart who is now as alone as you are. Connect with some friend of yours who lost a mate. Go to places where the other gender eat lunch. Go to exercise classes and lectures for seniors, art galleries, adult education classes, athletic events, parks, singles tours for seniors (send for brochure to SAGA holidays, 120 Boylston St., Boston, MA 02116 or call 1-800-248-2234).

10

Money Matters
Especially for Widows

Big Challenge

When your husband died, whatever was left to you in the way of material assets comprises your estate. Unless you are gainfully employed and/or have assets in your own right, this is what you and your family will have to live on. You should be seriously concerned with three things: <u>Preservation of your capital</u>—you cannot afford to lose it. <u>Income generation</u>—the highest rate consistent with reasonable risk. <u>Capital growth</u>—when we plant seeds, flowers, or trees, we expect them to grow.

This is a big order and is going to require considerable research on your part, but it will be worth it, because if your estate diminishes from year to year it will eventually be gone and you will not have the time or the opportunity to earn it again. Unless you have had previous experience and know your way around the investment field, this will be one of the most challenging and demanding tasks in your role as a widow. The world of personal finance is very complex and risky. To succeed in this area is not impossible, but you should not attempt to do it on your own.

There are many competent people in the financial world who would be willing to assist you. There is also a pack of wolves in sheep's clothing who want to get their hands on your assets and invest them wildly in all sorts of schemes. In the end they will have become wealthier through commissions they have made at your expense and you may end up being poorer. It's happening all the time, so BEWARE. It doesn't need to happen to you.

Get Help

One morning as I was leaving a bank where I do business, I ran into a treasured friend whose husband had passed away several months before and left her with about $600,000 in stocks and bonds. She did not know the difference between a stock certificate and a bond coupon. She had a whole bundle of these under her arm. She looked as though her whole world had blown apart, and in the loss of her husband, it had. She was the picture of harried confusion and bewilderment as she said, "Stan, I must find someone who can help me with all these things, because I just don't know the first thing about what to do with them." Apparently she had come to the right place, because over the years which followed, she learned to manage her estate acceptably, and when she died 15 years later, her estate was considerably larger than it was when it was first placed in her hands. Smart woman! It's always a wise decision when you make up your mind that you are going to find the best possible adviser to help you.

Road Signs

This chapter is not meant to be a complete course in wise investing. Instead, I would hope you would use it as a road map before you embark on some new, difficult, and dangerous terrain. It is my purpose to put up some signboards along the way, informing you of the safe roads to travel and also the unsafe ones which could lead to financial disaster.

After you have studied my suggestions, turn to the bibliography at the end of this book, find the section on "Money Matters," and make up your mind that before you do anything else you will commit yourself to reading some of the books listed there. Your local library has most of them.

The first one I would suggest is *Everyone's Money Book* by Jordan Goodman and Sonny Bloch. Don't let its size frighten you off. You don't need to read all of it, only the chapter on "Finding Financial Advisers Who Are Right for You," which is Chapter 18, and any other portions which pertain to your situation. This 1994 publication is very complete and gives good counsel.

It wouldn't be a bad idea to look into several others listed in the bibliography at the back of this book which might appeal to you. They essentially all give the same kind of advice. You will be amazed at how much fog and confusion melts away as you learn the principles of wise investing. Believe me, this can happen to you.

Second, write to the American Association of Retired Persons (AARP) Consumers Affairs Section, Program Coordination and Development Department, 601 E St., N.W., Washington, D.C. 20049, and ask for their free booklet, *Facts About Financial Planners*.

Third, make a trip to your local library and get AARP's magazine, *Modern Maturity,* for August-September 1993. Turn to page 45 and study the excellent article, "Risky Business—All Financial Planners Are Not Created Equal," by Mary Rowland.

Who Are the Financial Planners?

A listing of the many kinds of people who do financial planning resembles alphabet soup. Almost anyone can hang out a shingle with "financial planning" written on it. This profession is not highly regulated by law. The letters following the person's name indicate the degree of preparation that that person has had. But such a degree does not guarantee that that person is a successful planner. It only indicates that he or she has done some studying to learn the field. It is no guarantee of competence, nor is there a test to show how highly motivated that person would be in working for you.

In my opinion, one of the most competent planners in our city does not use a degree following his name. However, for many years he has been a successful real-estate broker, he drives a top-of-the-line car, he lives in a beautiful and expensive home in one of the finest neighborhoods of the city, and he is a millionaire. His own success is his credential.

Some hints of competence and interest might come out in your interview later and from clients the planner gives you as references. Be sure to ask for several references when you have your first interview.

AARP's *Modern Maturity* of August-September 1993 lists the following groups of financial planners:

CFP—Certified Financial Planner—this group is emerging as the most credible designation.

PFS—Personal Financial Specialist—certified public accountants.

CFA—Chartered Financial Analyst—must have completed a three-year program focusing on investment analysis.

CLU—Chartered Life Underwriter—specializes in insurance.

ChFC—Chartered Financial Consultant.

NAFCA—National Association of Personal Financial Advisers—work for a fee only.

RFP—Registry of Financial Practitioners—must hold CFA, CFP, ChFC, CPA. *Everyone's Money Book* (page 694) lists this group as "the cream of the financial planning crop."

Others

Stockbrokers and insurance people may also do financial planning. In dealing with these two groups, you must remember that both of them have a product to sell (stocks, bonds and insurance), and they are going to be pushing them. Be wary of the "one product" or "one company" planner. That is often a pattern for disaster. There is always a danger in putting all your eggs in one basket. It should also be said that approximately 80 percent of people in the financial planning arena have a product to sell in addition to giving you advice. Some planners are highly skilled, helpful, and attuned to your needs. Others are simply salesmen who care less about your financial goals than about generating commissions on the products they sell to you.

Banks: If you have a large sum of money to invest, it might be well for you to consider a bank. "If a bank offers a full line of banking, investment, insurance, and financial planning products and services, you might give it a try. It is certainly convenient to funnel most or all of your financial transactions through one institution, which can give you a complete monthly statement of where you stand. Banks offer a much higher level of service in their trust department, which you will never encounter if you merely walk into a branch. The trust department caters to wealthier customers with assets of at least $100,000 but usually $300,000 or more. Trust officers and their assistants are usually far more experienced and qualified to deal with your financial needs than bankers are. They offer in-depth financial and estate planning, tax preparation, insurance advice, and investment expertise (*Everyone's Money Book,* Goodman and Bloch, pages 691-692)."

Attorneys: In general practice, and especially tax attorneys.

Accountants and income tax preparers: A knowledgeable accountant can save you thousands of dollars in a way that minimizes the government's tax bite.

Sound Advice

The November 1987 AARP news bulletin quotes John Shad, then Securities and Exchange Commission chairman, at the previous year's congressional hearing on financial planners: "The first line of defense is the investor, and we would encourage them to look before they leap, to be skeptical." He then noted 10 points that he said are sound advice for anyone dealing with investment advisers:

1. Reject high-pressure telephone solicitations from strangers. (Slam down the phone on all unsolicited calls.)
2. Be very skeptical of promises of exceptional returns and profits. (If it's so easy to make big money, why isn't he doing it himself instead of telling me about it?)
3. Read financial planners' brochures—know their qualifications.
4. Before you invest, request and read the prospectuses and circulars that describe the investment.
5. Don't invest in something you don't understand. (Don't permit anyone to rush you into decisions without making sure you understand the details.)
6. Be wary of extremely low-priced penny stocks.
7. Don't put more money into high-risk investments than you can afford to lose.
8. Don't tie up most of your money in non-liquid investments.
9. Keep track of how your investments are doing.
10. If your financial planner refuses to give you information about your investments, or ignores your instructions, call your local Better Business Bureau, state securities regulator, or the SEC office.

You Don't Have to Fly Blind

Financial planning is one of the fastest-growing professions in the field of personal finance. There's a veritable army out there, maybe as many as 400,000 in our country.

If you find a good adviser and under his or her guidance you invest wisely, you will save money on taxes, insurance, and personal spending, and your assets will grow, rather than diminish. Ideally, a good financial planner should have the solution to everyone's financial problems. By looking at his client's financial resources, he can help formulate goals and come up with a plan to achieve them. He will evaluate areas of budget, insurance needs, investment plans, how to save on taxes, build retirement plans, and much more. Later on when you are interviewing prospective advisers, ask to see several plans each one has developed for other clients.

Where to Look

How does one find someone like this? Very often we find them in the same way we find a good lawyer, physician, tax-preparer or dentist. We ask our friends, relatives and colleagues. Not infrequently, there are free financial seminars advertised in the newspapers. It costs only a little time and effort to go and listen; you might discover someone whom you would like to take a second look at.

You might even ask your banker for a recommendation of someone who is not employed by his bank. Then there are the Yellow Pages in the phone book. If you still don't come up with anything that looks good to you, call the Institute for Certified Financial Planners at their toll-free number, 1-800-282-7526, and ask for a free copy of their brochure *Selecting a Financial Planner.* Their address is 7600 E. Eastman Ave., Suite 301, Denver, CO 80231.

After your first sweep of the field, you might come up with a dozen or more possibilities. But if you didn't, maybe you did not sweep far or long enough. Keep working at it, ask questions, and study until you have worked the list down to three or four with whom you would like to talk.

Make That Call

Now it's time to make a telephone call to each one and make certain that that person is on the other end of the line, not his secretary or someone else. Write notes as you ask a few questions, such as: How long have you been a financial planner in this community? What professional designations (letters following his name) do you have? How do you charge for your services—monthly flat fee, commission on what you sell, or a combination of the two? If the answer is "commissions" then ask, "How many firms do you represent? Will there be a charge for the first interview?" Most planners will be glad, or should be, to give half an hour or more to get acquainted and talk about your situation.

While this conversation is going on, think about your comfort level with this person. If most everything checks out on the plus side, make an appointment.

Old Story (for whatever it's worth!)

There's an old story about this situation which teaches you to try to get in on the first appointment of the day and get to the meeting place before he does. Presuming that you have already been introduced to him, if you see him drive up in an old jalopy or alight from public transportation, go home; don't keep the appointment. A man who cannot afford a better means of getting to work has no business being considered as your financial adviser; of course, it's possible that he or she is just very frugal. The same kind of reasoning applies to his dress code or lack of it.

The Interview

The April 17, 1994, *San Francisco Examiner* and *Chronicle* contained an excellent article, "To Find the Right Broker (Adviser) Ask Plenty of Questions." This article suggests the following questions:

1. How long have you been doing this kind of work, and what did you do prior to that?
2. What is your experience in working with clients like me?
3. What is your typical client like?
4. What is your educational background?
5. What credentials do you have for giving investment advice?
6. Do you have a specialty?
7. What is your investment approach (percentages of investments in stocks, bonds, cash)?
8. Have you ever had any complaints filed against you? If so, how were they resolved?
9. How often do you contact your clients?
10. How long does it take you to return telephone calls?
11. Who works with your clients when you are not available?
12. Are you paid from commissions only, a set fee, or a combination of both?
13. Will you recommend three current clients whom I can contact for references?

If you are purchasing securities (stocks, bonds, mutual funds, and partnerships), make certain your adviser is a Registered Investment Adviser (RIA) with the Securities and Exchange Commission. Part 2 of the form is available to clients—ask for it.

Following the interview, check up on what he or she told you—the three clients he gave as references and his educational background and work history. Make sure you get a written estimate of what services you can expect and at what price. Be wary of anyone who uses high-pressure tactics or promises unusually high rates of return. Remember, no investment is so good that you can't go home first to think it over. Anything that sounds too good to be true probably is too good to be true.

Even though you decide to employ a financial planner, you need to learn as much as you can about making wise investments so you can evaluate whether the planner's recommendations make sense for you. It is unwise to invest in something you don't understand. Because the financial scene is constantly changing, you cannot afford to expect a financial plan to take care of itself.

No one has as much at stake as you do in your finances. Just because you are working with a professional is no substitute for educating yourself about investments and taking responsibility for your investment decisions. Good advisers want their clients to understand what they are doing.

Continue reading, talking, and attending classes on money matters so you will learn when to consider making changes in your plan. This holds true even if you do not employ a planner.

In addition to looking into some of the suggestions in the bibliography, you should go to your local library and check out copies of *Money* magazine, *Changing Times, Consumer Reports, The Personal Investor,* and other financial magazines.

Danger

Some planners want discretionary control of their clients' funds, which allows the planner to invest as he or she sees fit. This arrangement is DANGEROUS! It is fraught with the potential of fraud and malfeasance. However, if for some strange reason you do agree to this, make certain that your planner is bonded. This should cover you in case he or she runs off with your money.

Millions of dollars have been lost this way. Remember, you cannot afford to lose what you have. Whenever changes are to be made in your portfolio, you are the one who should make the decision. Generally, it is not wise to employ a relative or friend to be your financial consultant.

Risk

Don't shy away from something just because it's risky. We do a great many things that are risky, like driving an automobile with so many crazy drivers on the road, falling in love and getting married, and then bringing children into our dangerous world and having to provide a home for them which we hope will be paid for in 30 years. We should be willing to take reasonable risks, because in doing so we might acquire what we want or need. "Take a chance—something good may happen. Take a chance—something bad may happen. Don't take a chance— nothing happens (Sophia and the "Golden Girls)." Any respected adviser will admit that the only way to achieve high returns over time is to take above-average risks.

In *Money Matters—Your IDS Guide to Financial Planning,* published by Avon Books, we find this good counsel: "Even without the benefit of hindsight, it's possible to make some judgment about the relative risk of various types of investments. As a rule, the more an investment's price fluctuates in value and the larger number of factors that can affect its price, the riskier it is. You should know that although risk-taking carries with it the potential of higher returns, wide price fluctuations make it impossible to count on achieving any specific return and increase the chances that you'll lose your principal (pages 17-18)."

Arrange to meet with your planner several times during the year. Ask for a complete report of your accounts. Should questions arise in your mind about any of your holdings, call your adviser and get a straight answer so you won't be worrying about it.

A good financial counselor will want to know his or her clients and listen to them. It is reasonable to believe that he is interested in a long-term relationship. The good counselor also educates his clients about investing and never downplays the risks or pressures them into decisions.

The Bottom Line

Don't do business with someone you are not comfortable with.

The final decision in making an investment must always be YOURS!

Support Groups That Offer Help

ALZHEIMER'S Disease and Related Disorders, Assoc. Inc.
360 N. Michigan Ave., Chicago, IL 60601
(Local chapters' addresses available upon request.)

American CANCER Society
219 E. 42nd St., New York, NY 10017

American HEART Association
44 E. 23rd St., New York, NY 10010

American LUNG Association
1740 Broadway, New York, NY 10019

CANCER CARE
1 Park Ave., New York, NY 10016

COMPASSIONATE FRIENDS
P.O. Box 3696, Oak Brook, IL 60522-3696
(For parents whose child has died.)

CANDLELIGHTERS Childhood Cancer Foundation
1901 Pennsylvania Ave. NW, Suite 1001, Washington, D.C. 20006

The DOUGY Foundation for Grieving Children
3039 SE 52nd St., Portland, OR 97206
(503) 775-5683

Families of HOMICIDE VICTIMS Program
c/o Victim Services Agency
2 Lafayette St., New York, NY 10007
(212) 577-7700
(Provides counseling for the surviving spouses of murder victims)

Mothers Against Drunk Drivers (M.A.D.D.)
669 Airport Freeway, Suite 310, Hurst, TX 76053
(817) 268-6233

National SUDDEN INFANT DEATH Foundation (SIDS)
310 S. Michigan Ave., Chicago, IL 60604
1-800-221-7437

PARENTS WITHOUT PARTNERS
8807 Colesville Road, Silver Spring, MD 20910
(301) 588-9354

Parents of MURDERED CHILDREN
100 East 8th St., Room B-41, Cincinnati, OH 45202
(513) 721-5683

SHARE (Source of Help in Airing and Resolving Experiences)
St. John's Hospital
800 East Carpenter, Springfield, IL 62769
(217) 544-6464

SIDS Alliance
1314 Bedford Ave., Suite 3210, Baltimore, MD 21208
1-800-221-SIDS

Society of MILITARY WIDOWS
5535 Hempstead Way, Springfield, VA 22151
(703) 750-1342

SURVIVORS OF SUICIDE
Suicide Prevention Center, Inc.
P.O. Box 1393, Dayton, OH 45401
(513) 223-9096

THEOS (They Help Each Other Spiritually)
1301 Clark Building, 717 Liberty Ave., Pittsburgh, PA 15222
(412) 471-7770

WIDOWED PERSONS Service
American Association of Retired Persons (AARP)
1909 K St., NW, Washington, D.C. 20049
(202) 872-7400

WIDOW'S NETWORK
3483 Golden Gate Way, Suite 2, Lafayette, CA 94549
(510) 283-7174

Bibliography

Some of the books listed are out of print and cannot be found in bookstores. However, they are excellent and might be found in your local public library.

For Children Who Have Lost a Loved One

Alderman, Linda. *Why Did Daddy Die?* New York: Pocket Books, 1989

Aldrich, Sandra. *Living Through The Loss of Someone You Love.* Ventura, CA: Regal Books, 1990 (Chapter 6)

Armstrong, William. *The Mills of God.* New York: Doubleday and Co., 1973 (11 years and up)

Berger, Terry. *I Have Feelings.* New York: Human Sciences Press, 1971 (ugly feelings are as valid as beautiful ones) (4-8 years)

Bernstein, Joanne. *Books to Help Children Cope with Separation and Loss.* New York: R. R. Bowker.

____. *Loss And How to Cope With It.* New York: Seabury Press, 1977 (middle school)

Bode, Janet. *Death Is Hard to Live With.* New York: Delacorte Press, 1993 (teens)

Boulden, Jim and Joan. *Saying Goodbye.* Santa Rosa, CA: Boulden Publishing Co. 1992 (3-7 years)

Brenner, Avis. *Helping Children Cope With Stress.* Lexington, MA: Lexington Books, 1984

Brown, M. W. *The Dead Bird.* New York: Young Scott Books, 1958

Buntin, Kathleen R. *When A Loved One Dies.* Salt Lake City, UT: Deseret Books, 1988

Bunting, Eve. *A Sudden Silence.* San Diego: Harcourt Brace Jovanovich, 1988 (older children)

Buscaglia, Leo. *The Fall of Freddie the Leaf.* New York: Charles B. Slack, 1982 (elementary school)

Clardy, Andrea. *Dusty Was My Friend.* New York: Human Sciences Press, 1984 (pre-school)

Cleaver, Vera and Bill. *Grover.* Philadelphia: Lippincott, 1970 (8-12 years)

Cleaver, Vera. *Where the Lilies Bloom.* Philadelphia: Lippincott, 1969

DePaola, Tomie. *Nana Upstairs and Nana Downstairs.* New York: Putnam, 1973 (K-8 grade)

Donnelley, Nina. *I Never Know What to Say.* New York: Ballantine, 1987 (Chapter 4)

_____. *Recovering From the Loss of a Sibling.* New York: Dodd, Mead & Co. 1988

_____. *Recovering From the Loss of a Parent.* New York: Berkeley Publishing, 1993

Fassler, Joan. *My Grandpa Died Today.* New York: Human Sciences Press, 1978 (under 8)

Furman, Erna. *A Child's Parent Dies.* New Haven, CT: Yale University Press, 1974

Gardner, Richard. *The Boys And Girls Book About Divorce.* New York: J. Avonson, 1983 (for parents and children meeting divorce together)

Gipson, Fred. *Old Yeller.* New York: Harper & Row, 1956

Gordon, Audrey K., and Klass, Dennis. *They Need to Know.* Englewood Cliffs, NJ: Prentice-Hall, 1979

Grollman, Earl. *Explaining Death to Children.* Boston: Beacon Press, 1967

_____. *Talking About Death*—A Dialogue Between Parent and Child. Boston: Beacon Press, 1970; 1976

_____. *Talking About Divorce.* Boston: Beacon Press, 1975; 1976

Hazen, Barbara. *Why Did Daddy Die?* New York: Golden Books, 1985

_____. *Why Did Grandpa Die?* New York: Golden Books, 1985 (pre-school and primary)

Jackson, Edgar N. *Telling A Child About Death.* New York: Channel Press, 1965

Jewett, Claudia. *Helping Children Cope With Separation and Loss.* Boston: Harvard Common Press, 1982; 1994 (adult)

Johnson, Joy and Marv. *Where's Jess?* Answers to a Little Girl's Questions about What Happened to Her Baby Sister. Omaha, NE: Centering Corp, 1982 (3-5 years)

Juneau, Barbara F. *Sad But O.K. My Daddy Died Today.* Nevada City, CA: Blue Dolphin Publishers, 1988 (elementary)

Krementz, Jill. *How It Feels When a Parent Dies.* New York: Alfred A. Knopf, 1988 (9-12 years)

Lee, Virginia. *The Magic Moth*—A Fictional Classic of Terminal Illness and Death Seen Through the Eyes of a Young Brother. New York: Seabury Press, 1972 (8-11 years)

LeShan, Eda. *Learning to Say Goodbye.* When a parent dies. New York: Macmillan & Co., 1976 (8-10 years)

Linn, Erin. *One Hundred Fifty Facts About Grieving Children.* Incline Village, New York: The Publisher's Mark, 1990

Lonetto, R. *Children's Conception of Death.* New York: Springer, 1980

Miles, Miska. *Annie and the Old One.* Boston: Little, Brown & Co., 1972

Rofes, Eric C. *The Kid's Book About Death and Dying.* Boston: Little, Brown & Co., 1985

Rando, Therese. *Grieving.* How to Go On Living When Someone You Love Dies. Lexington, MA: Lexington Books, 1988 (Chapter 13)

Richter, E. *Losing Someone You Love*—When a Brother or Sister Dies. New York: G.P. Putnam & Sons, 1986

Rogers, Fred. *When a Pet Dies.* New York: Putnam, 1988

Schaefer, Dan, and Lyons, Christine. *How Do We Tell The Children?* New York: Newmarket Press, 1986 (for parents)

Shector, Ben. *Someplace Else.* New York: Harper & Row, 1971 (8-12 years)

Smith, Doris Buchanan. *A Taste of Blackberries.* New York: Harper & Row, 1973 (7-10 years)

Smith, Harold Ivan. *Grieving the Death of a Father.* Minneapolis, MN: Augsburg, 1994

Staudacher, Carol. *Beyond Grief.* Oakland, CA: New Harbinger Publications, 1987 (Chapter 6)

Stein, Sarah B. *About Dying.* An open family book for parent and child. New York: Walker & Co., 1974 (3-6 years)

Tresselt, Alvin. *The Dead Tree.* New York: Parents Magazine Press, 1974 (8-12 years)

Vigna, Judith. *Saying Goodbye to Daddy.* Niles, Ill.: A. Whitman, 1991 (easy reader, pre-school)

Viorst, Judith. *The 10th Good Thing About Barney.* New York: Atheneum, 1971 (pre-school)

Vogel, Linda Jane. *Helping A Child Understand Death.* Philadelphia: Fortress Press, 1975

Wass, H., and C. Corr, eds. *Helping Children Cope With Death: Guidelines and Resources.* Washington, D.C.: Hemisphere, 1984

Wessel, M.A. *Medical Care of the Adolescent*—Adolescents and the Death of a Parent. New York: Appleton, Century Crafts, 1976 (Chapter 26)

White, E.B. *Charlotte's Web.* New York: Harper, 1952

Williams, Margery. *The Velveteen Rabbit.* Boston: David Godine, 1956

Wolf, Anna. *Helping Your Child to Understand Death.* New York: Child Study Press, 1973

Wolfelt, Alan. *Helping Children Cope With Grief.* Muncie, IN: Accelerated Development, Inc., 1983

For Those Who Are Divorced

Block, Jean Libman. *Back in Circulation*. New York: Macmillan, 1960

Gardner, Richard. *The Boys And Girls Book About Divorce*—For Parents of Children Meeting Divorce Together. New York: Bantam, 1971

Greteman, Jim. *Coping With Divorce*—From Grief to Healing. Notre Dame, IN: Ave Maria Press, 1981

Krantzler, Mel. *Creative Divorce*. New York: M. Evans & Co., 1973

____. *Learning To Love Again*. New York: Thomas W. Crowell, 1977

____. *Creative Marriage*. New York: McGraw-Hill, 1981

Petri, Darlene. *The Hurt and Healing of Divorce*. Elgin, IL: David C. Cook Publishing Co., 1976

Smoke, Jim. *Growing Through Divorce*. Irvine, CA: Harvest House Publishing Co., 1976

Stuart, Richard, and Jacobson, Barbara. *Second Marriage*. New York: W.W. Norton, 1985

Wallerstein, Judith S. *Surviving The Break-Up*. New York: Basic Books, 1980

Young, Amy Ross. *By Death or Divorce*—It Hurts to Lose. Denver: Accent Books, 1976

Helping Others

Bernstein, Joanne. *Books to Help Children Cope With Separation And Loss*. New York: R.R. Bowker, 1977; 1983; 1989

Donnelley, Nina. *I Never Know What To Say.* New York: Ballantine Books, 1987

Grollman, Earl. *In Sickness And In Health*. Boston: Beacon Press, 1987

Kolf, June C. *How Can I Help?* Grand Rapids, MI: Baker Book House, 1989

____. *When Will It Stop Hurting?* Grand Rapids, MI: Baker Book House, 1987

Kuenning, Delores. *Helping People Through Grief.* Minneapolis, MN: Bethany House Publishing Co., 1987

Klass, Dennis, and Gordon, Audrey. *They* [The Children] *Need to Know.* Englewood Cliffs, NJ: Prentice-Hall, 1979

Manning, Doug. *Comforting Those Who Grieve.* San Francisco: Harper & Row, 1985

Marletti, Leonard J. *When Someone You Know Has AIDS.* New York: Crown Publishers, 1987

Moffat, Betty Clare. *When Someone You Love Has AIDS.* Santa Monica, CA: IBS Press, 1986. Written by a mother of an AIDS victim

Schaefer, Dan, and Lyons, Christine. *How Do We Tell the Children?* A parents' guide. New York: Newmarket Press, 1986

Silverman, Phyllis. *Helping Each Other in Widowhood.* New York: Health Science Publishing Corp., 1974

Spingarn, Natalie D. *Hanging In There*—Living Well on Borrowed Time. New York: Stein & Day, 1983

Weizman, Savine G., and Karmm, Phyllis. *About Mourning*—Support and Guidance for the Bereaved. New York: Human Sciences Press, 1985

Worden, J. Wm. *Grief Counseling and Grief Therapy.* New York: Springer Publishing Co., 1982

Handling the Holidays

Conley, B. *Handling the Holidays.* Springfield, IL: Human Services Press, 1979; 1986

Grollman, Earl. *Time Remembered.* A Journal for Survivors. Boston: Beacon Press, 1987

Manning, Doug. *Grief and the Holidays.* Insight Books, Inc., Hereford, TX (P.O. Box 2058, 79045)

Woodson, Meg. *The Toughest Days of Grief.* Grand Rapids, MI: Zondervan Publishing Co., 1994

For Survivors of a Homicide or Death by Violence

Danto, B.L. *Survivors of Homicide*—The Human Side of Homicide. New York: Columbia University Press, 1982

Eisenberg, Hyman. *Inner Grief of Men.* Parents of Murdered Children, Inc., 100 E. 8th St., Suite 341, Cincinnati, OH 45202, 1993

Jensen, Amy H. *Healing Grief.* Redmond, WA: Medic Publishing Co. 1980

Lord, J. *No Time for Goodbyes.* Ventura, CA: Pathfinder Publishing, 1987

Rando, Therese (ed.). *Parental Loss of a Child.* Champaign, IL: Research Press, 1986

Ruhe-Munch, Nancy, and Rankin, Nancy. *Thanks for Asking.* A collection of remembrances for survivors by survivors. Cincinnati, OH: Parents of Murdered Children, Inc., 100 E. 8th St., Suite 341, Cincinnati, OH 45202, 1991

_____. *Sorrow of Siblings.* Siblings who have lost a brother or sister to murder. Parents of Murdered Children, Inc., 100 E. 8th St., Suite 341, Cincinnati, OH 45202, 1994

Miscellaneous References

Angel, M.D. *The Orphaned Adult*—A Guide for Adults. New York: Human Sciences Press, 1987

Bernstein, Joanne E. *Loss and How to Cope With It.* New York: Seabury Press, 1977

Boss, Pauline. *Ambiguous Loss—Learning to Live with Unresolved Grief.* Cambridge, MA: Harvard University Press, 1999

Colgrave, Melba, Bloomfield, H., McWilliams, Peter. *How to Survive the Loss of a Love.* New York: Bantam Books, 1981

Cornils, Stanley P. *The Mourning After*—How to Manage Grief Wisely. Grief Recovery, Vallejo, CA. 11th printing, 2002

Davidson, Glen. *Understanding Mourning.* Minneapolis, MN: Augsburg Publishing House, 1984

Donnelly, Katherine. *Recovering From the Loss of a Sibling.* New York: Dodd, Mead & Co., 1988

_____. *Recovering From the Loss of a Parent*—Adult Sons and Daughters Reveal How They Overcame Their Grief. New York: Dodd, Mead & Co., 1987

Fitzgerald, Helen. *The Mourning Handbook.* New York: Simon and Schuster, 1994

Glick, Ira O., Wise, Robert, and Parks, C. Murray. *The First Year of Bereavement.* New York: John Wiley & Sons, 1974

Greenwald, Jerry A. *Breaking Out of Loneliness.* New York: Warson, Wade Publishers, 1980

Grollman, Earl. *In Sickness and in Health*—How to Cope When Your Loved One Is Ill. Boston: Beacon Press, 1987

_____. *Living When a Loved One Has Died.* Boston: Beacon Press, 1977

Hulme, William E. *Creative Loneliness.* Minneapolis, MN: Augsburg Publishing Co., 1977

James, John W., and Cherry, Frank. *The Grief Recovery Handbook.* New York: Harper & Row, 1988

Kubler-Ross, Elisabeth. *On Death and Dying.* New York: Macmillan, 1969

Kushner, H.S. *When Bad Things Happen to Good People.* New York: Schocken Books, 1990

LeShan, Eda. *Learning to Say Goodbye*—When a Parent Dies. New York: Avon, 1976

Lewis, C.S. *A Grief Observed.* New York: Bantam Books, 1963

Liebman, Joshua Loth. *Peace of Mind.* New York: Simon & Schuster, 1946

Lynch, James. *The Broken Heart*—The Medical Consequences of Loneliness. New York: Basic Books, 1977

Manning, Doug. *What to Do When You Lose a Loved One.* San Francisco: Harper & Row, 1984

_____. *Don't Take My Grief Away.* New York: Harper & Row, 1984

Morris, Sarah. *Grief and How to Live With It.* New York: Grosset & Dunlap, 1972

Myers, Edward. *When Parents Die*—A Guide for Adults. New York: Viking, 1986

Neeld, Elizabeth Harper. *Seven Choices*—Taking the Steps to New Life after Losing Someone You Love. New York: Clarkson N. Potter, Inc., 1990

O'Connor, Nancy. *Letting Go With Love.* Apache Junction, AZ: La Mariposa Press, 1984

Price, Eugenia. *Getting Through the Night*—Finding Your Way after the Loss of a Loved One. New York: Dial Press, 1982

Rando, Therese. *Grieving:* How to Go On Living When Someone You Love Dies. Lexington, MA: Lexington Books, 1988

_____. *How to Go On Living When Someone You Love Dies.* Same book as above in soft cover. New York: Bantam Books, 1991

Rank, Maureen. *Free to Grieve.* Minneapolis, MN: Bethany House Publishers, 1985

Raphael, Beverly. *The Anatomy of Bereavement.* New York: Basic Books, 1983

Schiff, Harriet S. *Living Through Mourning.* New York: Penguin Books, 1986

Shahan, Lynn. *Living Alone and Liking It.* New York: Warner Books, Inc., 1981

Shaw, Eva. *What to Do When a Loved One Dies.* Irvine, CA: Dickens Press, 1994

Slaikeu, K., and Lawhead, S. *Up From the Ashes:* Surviving and Growing Through Crisis. Grand Rapids, MI: Zondervan Publishing Co., 1987 (first published as The Phoenix Factor, Houghton Mifflin, 1985)

Staudacher, Carol. *Beyond Grief.* Oakland, CA: Harbinger Publications, 1987

Stearns, Ann Kaiser. *Living Through Personal Crisis.* New York: Ballantine Books, 1984

Stringfellow, William A. *A Simplicity of Faith*—My Experience in Mourning. Nashville, TN: Abingdon Press, 1982

Tatelbaum, Judy. *The Courage to Grieve.* New York: Harper and Row, 1980

_____. *You Don't Have to Suffer.* New York: Harper & Row, 1989

Tauris, Carol. *Anger.* New York: Simon & Schuster, 1982

Veninga, Robert. *A Gift of Hope.* Boston: Little, Brown & Co., 1985

Walker, Harold B. *To Conquer Loneliness.* New York: Harper & Row

Westberg, Granger E. *Good Grief.* Philadelphia: Fortress Press, 1962

Woodson, Meg. *The Toughest Days of Grief.* Grand Rapids, MI: Zondervan Publishing Co., 1994

Worden, J.W. *Grief Counseling and Grief Therapy.* New York: Springer, 1982

_____. *Understanding Grief.* Fort Collins, CO., Companion Press, 1992

Young, Ann L. *By Death or Divorce—It Hurts to Lose.* Denver, CO: Accent Books, 1976

Pet Loss

Anderson, Moira K. *Coping With The Sorrow After the Loss of a Pet.* Los Angeles: Peregrine Press, 1987

Brown, Margret. *The Dead Bird.* Reading, MA: Addison Wesley, 1976 (primary)

Carrick, Carol. *The Accident.* New York: Clarion, 1976 (primary)

_____. *The Foundling.* New York: Clarion, 1977 (primary)

Cusak, O. *Pets and the Elderly.* New York: Haworth Press, 1983

Greenberg, Judith. *Sunny: The Death of a Pet.* New York: F. Watts, 1986

Kay, W.J., et al. *Pet Loss And Human Bereavement.* Ames, IA: Iowa State University Press, 1984

Miles, Betty. *The Trouble With Thirteen.* New York: Avon Books, 1980 (elementary)

Miles, Miska. *Annie and the Old One.* Boston: Little, Brown & Co., 1971

Nieberg, H.A., and Fischer, A. *Pet Loss.* New York: Harper & Row, 1982

Quackenbush, Jamie. *When Your Pet Dies.* New York: Simon & Schuster

Sussman, M. (ed.). *Pets and the Family.* New York: Haworth Press, 1985

Thomas, Jane R. *The Comeback Dog.* New York: Haworth Press, 1981 (elementary)

Viorst, Judith. *The Tenth Good Thing About Barney.* New York: Atheneum Publishers, 1971 (primary)

Wilhelm, Hans. *I'll Always Love You.* New York: Crown Publishers, 1985 (primary)

For Parents Who Have Lost a Child

Bayly, Joseph. *The Last Thing We Talk About.* Elgin, IL: David C. Cook, 1969

Bordow, Joan. *The Ultimate Loss.* New York: Beaufort Books, Inc., 1982

Borg, Susan, and Lasker, Judith. *When Pregnancy Fails.* Boston: Beacon Press, 1981

Bramblett, John. *When Goodbye Is Forever.* New York: Ballantine Books, 1991

Cook, J.A. *If I Should Die Before I Wake*—Religious Commitment and Adjustment to the Death of a Child. Journal for the Scientific Study of Religion, 22(3), pp. 222-238

Donnelly, Katherine. *Recovering from the Loss of a Child.* New York: Macmillan, 1982

Grotenhuis, Eleanor. *Song of Triumph.* Grand Rapids, MI: Baker Book House, 1991

Johnson, Joy and Marv. *Newborn Death.* Omaha, NE. Centering Corporation, 1982

Knapp, Ronald. *Beyond Endurance*—When a Child Dies. New York: Schocken Books, 1986

Kuhlman, Edward. *An Overwhelming Interference.* Old Tappan, NJ: Fleming R. Revell, 1986

Kushner, Harold S. *When Bad Things Happen to Good People.* New York: Avon, 1981

Munday, John and Frances. *Surviving the Death of a Child.* Louisville, KY: John Knox, 1995

Quezada, Adolfo. *Goodbye My Son, Hello.* St. Meinrad, IN: Abbey Press, 1985

Rando, Therese A. (ed.) *Parental Loss of a Child.* Champaign, IL: Research Press, 1986

Rosos, Barbara. *The Worst Loss.* New York: Henry Holt & Co., 1994

Schiff, Harriett. *The Bereaved Parent.* New York: Crown Publishers, 1977

Schatz, William H. *Healing a Father's Grief.* Redmond, WA: Medical Publishing Co., 1984

Speiss, Margaret. *Cries from the Heart.* Grand Rapids, MI: Baker Book House, 1991

Tengbom, Mildred. *Help for Bereaved Parents.* St. Louis: Concordia Publishing Co., 1981

Vredevelt, Pam. *Empty Arms.* Portland, OR: Multnomah Press, 1984

Wolterstorff, Nicholas. *Lament for a Son.* Grand Rapids, MI: Wm. B. Eerdmans Publishing Co., 1987

Remarriage

Belovitch, Jeanne. *Making Re-Marriage Work.* Lexington, MA: D.C. Heath & Co., 1987

Bernard, Jessie. *Remarriage.* New York: Russell & Russell, 1971

Cowan, Connell, and Kinder, Melvyn. *Smart Women, Foolish Choices.* New York: Clarkson N. Potter, 1985

Hanson, Dian. *How to Pick Up a Man.* New York: G.P. Putnam & Sons, 1982

Janda, Louis, and McCormack, Ellen. *The Second Time Around*—Why Some Marriages Fail While Others Succeed. New York: Carol Publishing Group, 1991

Karm, Phyllis. *Remarriage*—In the Middle Years and Beyond. San Leandro, CA: Bristol Publishing Enterprises, 1991

Krantzler, Mel. *Creative Marriage.* New York: McGraw-Hill, 1981

_____. *Learning to Love Again.* New York: Thomas T. Crowell Co., 1977

Kreis, Bernardine. *To Love Again:* An Answer to Loneliness. New York: Seabury Press, 1975

Lorimer, Ann, and Feldman, Philip. *Remarriage*—A Guide for Singles, Couples, and Families. Philadelphia: Running Press, 1980

Maddox, Brenda. *The Half-Parent.* New York: M. Evans & Co., 1975

McConnell, Adeline, and Jacobson, Barbara. *Single After 50.* New York: McGraw-Hill, 1978 (especially Chapters 8—What Men Find Attractive in Women Over 60, and 15—So You Think You Want to Get Married Again—How to Know)

Messinger, Lillian. *Remarriage*—A Family Affair. New York: Plenum Press, 1984

Nobel, June and William. *How to Live With Other People's Children.* New York: Hawthorne Books, 1977

Steward, Markabell Young. *The New Etiquette Guide to Getting Married Again.* New York: St. Martin's Press, 1980

Stuart, Richard B., and Jacobson, Barbara. *Second Marriage*—Make It Happy—Make It Work. New York: W.W. Norton & Co., 1985

Walker, Glynnis. *Second Wife, Second Best?* Managing Your Marriage as a Second Wife. Garden City, New York: Doubleday & Co., 1984

Weber, Eric. *The Divorced Woman's Guide to Meeting New Men.* New York: William Morrow & Co., 1984

Westoff, Leslie Aldridge. *The Second Time Around.* New York: Penguin Books, 1977

For Those Who Have Experienced Loss From SIDS, Stillbirth, Miscarriage, Neo-Natal Death

Borg, Susan, and Lasker, Judith. *When Pregnancy Fails.* Boston: Beacon Press, 1981

DeFrain, John. *Stillborn*—The Invisible Death. Lexington, MA: Lexington Books, 1986

DeFrain, John, Taylor, Jacque, and Ernst, Linda. *Coping With Sudden Infant Death.* Lexington, MA: Lexington Books, 1982

Ewy, Donna and Rodger. *Death of a Dream:* Miscarriage, Stillbirth, and Newborn Loss. New York: E.P. Dutton, 1984

Horchler, Joani, and Mossis, Robin Rice. *The SIDS Survival Guide.* Hyattsville, MD: SIDS Educational Services, 1994

Ilse, Sherokee, and Burns, Linda. *Miscarriage.* Long Lake, MN: Wintergreen Press, 1985

Panuthos, Claudia, and Romeo, Catherine. *Ended Beginnings*—Healing Child Bearing Loss. South Hadley, MA: Bergin & Garvey, 1984

Peppers, Larry G., and Knapp, Ronald J. *How to Go On Living after the Death of a Baby.* Atlanta: Peachtree Publishers, Ltd. 1985

Pizer, Hank, and O'Brien Palmiski, Christine. *Coping with a Miscarriage.* New York: New American Library, 1980

Rank, Maureen. *Free to Grieve.* Minneapolis, MN: Bethany House Publishers, 1985

Vredevelt, Pam W. *Empty Arms*—Stillbirth. Portland, OR: Multomah Press, 1984

For Survivors of Suicide

Alvarez, A. *The Savage God*—A Study of Suicide. New York: Bantam Books, 1972

Blackburn, Bill. *What You Should Know About Suicide.* Waco, TX: Word Books, 1982

Bolton, A., and Mitchell, C. *My Son—My Son*—A Guide to Healing After a Suicide. Atlanta: Bolton Press, 1983

Bowden, Susan White. *Everything to Live For.* New York: Harper & Row, 1987

Cain, Albert C. *Survivors of Suicide.* Springfield, IL: Charles Thomas, 1972

Chance, Sue. *Healing After Loss.* New York: Avon Books, 1994

Clemens, James T. (ed.) *Sermons On Suicide.* Louisville, KY: Westminster Press, 1989

Griffen, Mary, and Felsenthal, Carol. *A Cry for Help.* New York: Doubleday, 1983 (a guide for parents of adolescents)

Grollman, Earl. *Suicide.* Boston: Beacon Press, 1971.

Hewett, John. *After Suicide.* Philadelphia: Westminster Press, 1980.

Klagsbrun, Francine. *Too Young to Die*—Youth And Suicide. Boston: Houghton Mifflin, 1976. New York: Pocket Books, 1977

Leonard, Calista. *Understanding and Preventing Suicide.* Springfield, IL: Charles C. Thomas, 1974

Lester, Gene and David. *Suicide—The Gamble With Death.* Englewood Cliffs, NJ: Prentice-Hall, 1972

Linzer, Norman (ed.) *Suicide:* The Will to Live vs the Will to Die. New York: Human Sciences Press, 1983

Lukas, Christopher. *Silent Grief*—Living in the Wake of Suicide. New York: Macmillan, 1987

Miller, John. (ed.) *On Suicide.* San Francisco: Chronicle Books, 1992

Nelson, Robert E., Jr. *W.I.N.N. Against Suicide.* San Jose, CA: R & E Publishers, 1994

Overley, Patricia Harness. *A Message of Hope.* New York: Doubleday, 1990

Peck, Michael L., and Farbero, Norman. *Youth Suicide.* New York: Springer Publishing Co., 1985

Ross, Eleanora. *After Suicide*—A Ray of Hope. Springfield, IL: Creative Marketing, 1981

Shneidman, Edwin, and Farbero, Norman. *Some Facts About Suicide.* New York: Springer Publishing Co., 1985

Smolin, Ann, and Guinan, John. *Healing After the Suicide of a Loved One.* St. Louis: Fireside, 1993

Staudacher, Carol. *Beyond Grief.* Oakland, CA: Harbinger Publications, 1989

Stone, Howard. *Suicide and Grief.* Philadelphia: Fortress Press, 1972

Tatelbaum, Judy. *The Courage to Grieve.* New York: Harper & Row, 1980

Throop, John R. *Dealing With Suicide.* Elgin, IL: David C. Cook, 1989

For Those Whose Loved One Is Terminally Ill

Adams, D., and Deveau, E. *Coping With Childhood Cancer.* Ontario, Canada: Kinbridge Publications, 1984

Bluebond-Langner, M. *The Private Worlds of Dying Children.* Princeton, NJ: Princeton University Press, 1978

Burnham, Betsy. *When Your Friend Is Dying.* Grand Rapids, MI: Chosen Books, 1982

Carroll, David. *Living With Dying.* New York: McGraw-Hill, 1985

Cohen, D., and Eisdorfer, C. *Family Handbook on Alzheimer's Disease.* New York: W.H. Freeman, 1983

Davidson, Glen W. *Living With Dying.* Minneapolis, MN: Augsburg Publication House, 1975

Dobihal, Edward F., Jr., and Stewart, Charles W. *When a Friend is Dying.* Nashville, TN: Abingdon Press, 1984

Doka, Kenneth J. (ed.). *Living with Grief When Illness Is Prolonged.* Washington, D.C.: Hospice Foundation of America, 1997

Grollman, Earl A. *When Your Friend is Dying*. Boston: Beacon Press, 1980

Hutschnecker, Arnold L. *The Will to Live*. Englewood Cliffs, NJ: Prentice-Hall, 1951

Kopp, Ruth. *When Someone You Love is Dying*. Grand Rapids, MI: Zondervan Publishing House, 1980

Kubler-Ross, Elisabeth. *On Death and Dying*. New York: Macmillan, 1969

LeShan, Eda. *Learning to Say Goodbye*. New York: Macmillan, 1976

Mace, Nancy L., and Rabins, Peter. *The 36 Hour Day*. Baltimore, MD, and London: Johns Hopkins University Press, 1981

Martelli, Leonard J. *When Someone You Know Has AIDS*. New York: Crown Publishers, 1987

McGowan, Diana. *Living in the Labyrinth*. New York: Dell Publishing, 1993 (Alzheimer's)

Rando, Therese. *Grief, Dying and Death*—Clinical Interventions for Caregivers. Champaign, IL: Research Press, 1984

_____. *Loss and Anticipatory Grief*. Lexington, MA: Research Press, 1984

Robertson, John. *The Rights of the Critically Ill*. New York: Bantam Books, 1983

Shepard, Martin. *Someone You Love Is Dying*. New York: Harmony House, 1975

Smedes, Lewis. *How Can It Be All Right When Everything Is All Wrong?* San Francisco: Harper & Row, 1982

Weisman, Avery D. *On Dying and Denying*—A Psychiatric Study on Terminality. New York: Behavioral Publications, Inc., 1972

For the Widowed

Block, Jean Libman. *Back in Circulation*. New York: Macmillan, 1969

Brothers, Joyce. *Widowed*. New York: Simon & Schuster, 1990

Caine, Lynn. *Lifelines*. Garden City, New York: Doubleday, 1978

_____. *Being A Widow.* New York: Arbor House, 1988

Campbell, Scott, and Silverman, Phyllis. *Widowers.* New York: Prentice-Hall, 1987

Cornils, Stanley P. *The Mourning After*—How to Manage Grief Wisely. 11th printing, Vallejo, CA: Grief Recovery, 2002

Fisher, Ida, and Lane, Byron. *The Widow's Guide to Life.* Long Beach, CA: Lane-Con Press, 1985

Gordon, Beverly. *The First Year Alone.* Dublin, NH: W.L. Bauhan, 1986

Grollman, Earl A. *Living When a Loved One Has Died.* Boston: Beacon Press, 1977

Ginsburg, Genevieve D. *To Live Again.* Los Angeles: Jeremy P. Tarcher, 1987

Kohn, Jane B., and Willard, K. *The Widower.* Boston: Beacon Press, 1976

Kushner, Harold S. *When Bad Things Happen to Good People.* New York: Avon Books, 1981

Marshall, Catherine. *To Live Again.* New York: McGraw-Hill, 1957

Miller, Yolanda. *You Can Become Whole Again.* Atlanta: John Knox Press, 1981

Morris, Sarah. *Grief and How to Live with It.* New York: Grosset & Dunlap, 1972

Nudel, Adele Rice. *Starting Over*—Help for Young Widows and Widowers. New York: Dodd, Mead & Co., 1986

Nye, Mariam. *But I Never Thought He'd Die.* Philadelphia: Westminster Press, 1978

O'Conner, Nancy. *Letting Go With Love.* Apache Junction, AZ: La Mariposa Press, 1984

Shultz. *Widows, Wise and Otherwise.* Philadelphia and New York: Lippincott Co., 1949

Silverman, William B., and Cinnamon, Kenneth M. *When Mourning Comes.* Chicago: Nelson-Hall, 1981

Start, Clarissa. *When You're a Widow.* St. Louis: Concordia, 1968

Stearns, Ann Kaiser. *Living Through Personal Crisis.* Chicago: The Thomas Moore Press, 1984

Tatelbaum, Judy. *The Courage to Grieve.* New York: Harper & Row, 1980

____. *You Don't Have to Suffer.* New York: Harper & Row, 1989

Veninga, Robert L. *A Gift of Hope*—How We Survive Our Tragedies. New York: Ballantine Books, 1985

Westberg, Granger. *Good Grief.* Philadelphia: Fortress Press, 1971

Wylie, Betty Jane. *The Survival Guide for Widows.* New York: Ballantine Books, 1982 (formerly published as *Beginnings—A Book for Widows.*)

Money Matters

Briles, Judith. *The Woman's Guide to Financial Savvy.* New York: St. Martin's Press, 1981

Brown, Judith N., and Baldwin, Christina. *A Second Start—A Widow's Guide to Financial Survival.* New York: Simon & Schuster, 1986

Fowler, Elizabeth M. *Every Woman's Guide to Profitable Investing.* New York: American Management Association, 1986

Goodman, Jordan E., and Bloch, Sonny. *Everyone's Money Book.* Chicago: Dearborn Publishing Co., 1994

Goodman, George (Smith, Adam). *The Money Game.* New York: Random House, 12th printing, 1968

Graham, Benjamin. *The Intelligent Investor.* New York: Harper & Row, 1973

IDS Financial Services. *Money Matters—Your IDS Guide to Financial Planning.* New York: Avon Books, 1990

Klott, Gary L. *The New York Times Complete Guide to Personal Investing.* New York: New York Times Books, 1987

Porter, Sylvia. *Sylvia Porter's Money Book for the 80's.* New York: Avon Books, 1980

Siverd, Bonnie. *Count Your Change—A Woman's Guide to Sudden Financial Change.* New York. Arbor House, 1983

Slegel, Jack G., and Shinn, Jae K. *Investments: A Self Teaching Guide.* New York: John Wiley and Sons, Inc., 1986

Tobias, Andrew. *The Only Investment Guide You'll Ever Need.* New York: Harcourt Brace Jovanovich, 1978

Weaver, Peter and Annette. *What to Do With What You've Got.* Glenview, IL: AARP/Scott, Foresman, 1984